Diary of L.S.T. 351

Through the Lens of a Machinist Mate

(March 28, 1943 – December 19, 1944)

By
Albert Emil Klumpp

Transcribed by
Thelma Klumpp & Donna Rahn

ISBN: 9781705617441

Non-Exclusive Rights for Text Use Inside Book

Melville B. Grosvenor, National Geographic Image Collection #972081

Library of Congress Control Number: 2020903666

DEDICATION

In loving memory of Albert Emil Klumpp
July 24, 1921 - October 14, 2001

This book of Al's Diary is dedicated to Mikael, my grandson, who at a very young age, was truly fascinated by his great grandfather, Albert E. Klumpp. Mike wanted to know all about the time his grandfather spent serving his country, during WWII. Mikael would always ask to see the pictures, metals and memorabilia that had been stored in a plastic tub until he was old enough to really appreciate them. To Mikael these souvenirs were very special to him. When he was around 5 years old, he would take out each item as if it was a piece of gold, and he would ask his great grandmother to tell him about it. To Mikael these WWII items were his grandfather, Albert E. Klumpp – the grandfather he never knew.

Donna Rahn

INTRODUCTION

This project started (as a vision) in 2004 by, Al's wife, Thelma, she was inspired by her great grandson, Mikael. The project quickly became a passion to turn Al's Diary from his experiences on the L.S.T. during WWII into a book of memories for Mikael. No one in the family knew that Al kept a daily log of events (except Thelma), leading up to the invasion of Normandy. It took over 10 years for Thelma to transcribe Al's diary to their daughter and only child, Donna. Thelma would read the diary over the phone to Donna. Then Donna would type it on her computer. They could only do a few hours at a time because Al's handwriting was so hard to read. The weeks turned into months and months would turn into years until the project was finally finished in 2019.

During the long hours on the phone dictating, there were many laughs and tears along this journey, but Thelma always felt it was worth all the effort. They would have created a primary source of Al's experiences and thoughts during his time on the L.S.T. which they could share with others. Thelma loved telling her friends what she and Donna were doing and how much time they were spending together on it. Her hope was that when completed she would have something really special to give to Mikael, (their only great grandson) and to Tony and Scott, (their grandsons). Little did she know that she would be creating a document for the archives of American History.

Thelma gave a small pocket knife from Al's collection to Scott, (Mike's dad). After Mikael saw it, he asked where it came from. When he found out it was his great grandfathers', he asked "where are my presents from great grandpop"? Didn't he leave me anything?" That started a lot of questions about, Al's war memorabilia and his great grandfather's time in the war. He would constantly ask Thelma to see everything that was stored in a large tub. He became very interested; almost obsessed by the items. Thelma thought it only fitting to make him a small box of token things from Al's collection. Mikael's interest was the key motivation for Thelma to do this special project.

Even though Mikael was only a little over a year old when Al passed, he loved Mikael dearly and was very proud of his only great grandson. Al loved to take pictures of him and now Mike has those special pictures to look back on.

I thank my mom, Thelma for having the vision for this book. It was such a labor of love for both of us, an opportunity I would have not been able to complete without her. What a legacy, to have a first-person account of the historical events during WWII leading up to the invasion of Normandy. Even though, US Military Regulations prohibits any servicemen from keeping a personal log. Al's diary was written with full knowledge of the skipper who would ask Al to look up what maneuvers were done from the previous day, so that the information would be entered accurately in the ships log.

Unfortunately, my mom passed on Nov. 6, 2011 before she could see the diary completed. I needed to see this project completed to honor both her memory and my dad.

Al's first love was "Thelm" as he called her. They did everything together. They were a single unit and enjoyed life to the fullest. He loved waiting on her everyday of their married life. While in the service, he wrote love letters to her, which she kept in a shoebox. Later in life they traveled, and did travel-logs that were produced by Al himself, that was his passion from their many trips. He was also known for hosting many memorable holiday parties with family and friends.

Al was very proud of both of his grandsons, who he referred to as my Number 1 grandson, Tony and number 2 grandson Scott. He loved their passion for life and loved when they called him for advice. He could spend hours on the phone answering their questions. He would also take them on various day trips, shared his knowledge, and good values to live by. They both have such fond memories and many good laughs when they look back on those times.

Al would also, love to spar with Henry, his son-in-law over who was better, Navy or Army because Henry served in the Army. Al told him the Navy had better food, that is the main reason he joined the Navy. They also like talking about their careers and politics; which usually got a little heated, since they both had a German background. Al's favorite saying was " I may not always be right, but I'm never wrong."

Al's passion for life included photography and computers. He loved taking pictures of all kinds, especially wildlife. He joined the Camera Club in Moorestown NJ where he held every position on the board of directors and won every award possible for his beautiful pictures. He loved to mentor future photographers. He would really light up when he was the presenter and loved having his work judged by his peers. He also was a photographer for *The News Chronicle*, their local newspaper in his hometown of Moorestown. He was a lithographer by trade and worked in Philadelphia, Pennsylvania until he retired.

Long before the digital age, he used large commercial cameras. He would bring home projects like baseball cards that came with bubble gum. These cards were printed on one large sheet and had to be cut to size He also, printed beautiful landscapes that were done for advertising clients. He continued this passion through out his life, with an incredible zest for knowledge. He never could get enough! He would go to bed thinking of a problem so that he had something to work on the next day. When Digital cameras were introduced, he picked one up and loved the new technology. If you asked him how he was feeling he would always tell you….. "never better".   We all miss him so much, and thank him for all the memories and knowledge he gave each one of us over the years. We will always love you Dad.

The entries ended on December 19,1944; Al arrived home December 24, 1944 surprising Thelma, family and friends on Christmas Eve. Later they had a big surprise party for him at his parents' home in Philadelphia, where he got engaged to Thelma. They were married over 50 years and lived in Moorestown, NJ with their daughter.

I truly hope, those who read this book, will enjoy it and come away with a new appreciation for the events during that time in history. Al was a special, person with a zest for life. He will be in our hearts forever. We thank you Dad, for your years of service, and to all Veterans who have or are serving to protect our country.

L.S.T. 351

Landing **Ship**, Tank (**LST**), or tank landing **ship**, is the naval designation for **ships** first developed during World War II (1939-1945) to support amphibious operations by carrying tanks, vehicles, cargo, and landing troops directly onto shore with no docks or piers. They were fondly called "Large Slow Targets" by the crew.

Wikipedia

March-28-1943 Sunday - Solomon's, MD

From barracks #9, in the Solomon's, Maryland, we left for Washington, D.C. We went by bus at 13.00. It was a clear cool day. Our bus was first to arrive. Al MacIntyre, Richard Grant, Halbraum, Craig and others had one hour before train departure in which to see Washington. After buying some small trinkets, we boarded our train and headed toward Philly. We laid over North Philly Station for a quarter of an hour. We stopped directly over Broad St. We than made our way through Philly, past Frankford and other sections of our city and then headed toward NJ. After passing through Newark, we then pulled into Grand Central Station. Instead of boarding our ship we were taken to Pier #92, the worst place that I have ever been in my life. We did not unpack. We slept in our dress clothes and most fellows walked the floor all night to keep warm and to protect their belongings. I, of course, slept.

March-29-1943 Monday - Bayonne, NJ

This day we got our things together and were taken to Bayonne, NJ. We found our ship here. It was a new L.S.T.

March-30-1943 Tuesday - Bayonne, NJ

I stood my first watch. It was in the port troop compartment. That night we were invited to the Hotel Plaza. It was an affair given for our flotilla. I went with Kipley and Kenny. Kep got separated from us and Kenny and I continued on together.

March-31-1943 Wednesday - Philadelphia Naval Shipyard

After the six of us, the new firemen, painted the officer's quarters, we were given Liberty. I arrived home at 24.30, that night. I sat and talked with mother, Dad and Ed (Al's brother), before retiring.

March-32-1943 Thursday *(as written wrong date)* **- Philadelphia Naval Shipyard**

I visited Lt. Forsyth in the Wiedner Bldg. I also visited Ens. Hunter, Lt. Commander Holt, Lt. Borlick, Chief Grieves, all of the Philadelphia Navy Yard.

April-3-1943 Saturday - Philadelphia Naval Shipyard

Today our Liberty expires. I met Johnson and others at 0:400 at Philadelphia Station and proceeded to our ship.

April-10-1943 Saturday - Philadelphia Naval Shipyard

Between April 3 to the 10th our ship was being completed at Todds. Today we left for Brooklyn to have our L.C.T. (Landing Craft Tank) put on. This took two hrs. after which time we returned to Todds.

April-11-1943 Sunday - Philadelphia Naval Shipyard

Workers are finishing their jobs.

April-12-1943 Monday - Philadelphia Naval Shipyard

Today I was given our pay accounts and took them to Pier 45. After straightening our pay accounts I was granted special liberty to the next morning.

April-13-1943 Tuesday - Philadelphia Naval Shipyard

We left for Pier 42, where we took on medical soldiers.

April-14-1943 Wednesday - At Sea

We left Pier 42 for sea. It was early in the morning when we passed the Statue of Liberty; we then joined our convoy.

April-15-1943 Thursday - At Sea

The water got quite rough and sea sickness occurred.

April-17-1943 Saturday – Bermuda

Up to this date we had no trouble. We arrived at Bermuda. It was late in the afternoon when we reached there.

Al in L.S.T. 351 Engine Room

L.S.T. ENGINE ROOM

AL

CREW L.S.T.351

L.S.T. CREW'S QUARTERS

April-18-1943 Sunday - Bermuda

At 05.00 we got up and went to shore. We landed at a Naval aircraft base, only 1/2 a mile away. After landing I met, Grant, George and others. We all got aboard, Army trucks and traveled to a distant target range, over looking the ocean. We traveled about 15 miles through winding roads to one of the highest points in Bermuda. We practiced in 20's (caliber) and 40's (caliber). We then ate our lunch high above sea level with Ens. Myers. During chow a native of Bermuda came through in a cart drawn by a horse selling soda, candy and cakes.(Way profitable for him because we bought him out.) We then continued our practicing. We shot at a sleeve damaged by a plane. We then proceeded back to our ship. The native life of Bermuda is very simple. They keep their homes and gardens in very good conditions. Bicycling is the chief mean of transportation. The only cars there were operated by the Army. As our ship was lying in a bay we could see much of the Mainland. From our ship we could trace their quaint trolley line. It consisted of three cars, first, second, and third class cars. It wound itself among the hills and across small bridges. It was more effective at night to watch the light of the train moving among the distant hills. At our distance it looked like a toy. The climate was nice and warm because of the Gulf Stream. Their water is not very good for drinking because of this they catch rain water and purify it. They catch it by big domes.

April-20-1943 Tuesday - Bermuda

We did very little this day except swim.

April-20-1943 Tuesday At Sea heading to Africa

Today we weighed anchor and headed due East in a convoy of 80 ships. We then knew we were going to Africa.

April-20-1943 Tuesday At Sea heading to Africa

The sea once again became rough and sickness came in view again.

May-3-1943 Monday - At Sea

During the last few days very little has happened, except for sub activity.
Fortunately nothing happened.

May-4-1943 Tuesday - At Sea going to Casablanca

We are now NE. Before this we were traveling SE to avoid the Canary Islands and Madeira Island, which lies due East of Bermuda and West of Casablanca. We left one half of our convoy and this time to go to Casablanca, which lies on the West coast of Africa. We then sailed NE up the coast.

May-5-1943 Wednesday - Straits of Gibraltar

I was on watch from 24.00-08.00. I was one of the first to site the coming of the straits of Gibraltar. We passed through the straits during our general quarters, which are held at sunrise and sunset. We sited many schools of porpoises in this region. This night we were on best of guard in this region.

May-6-1943   09.00 Thursday - Nemours, Africa

 Today we pulled into a small French town called Nemours. It lies 150 miles from Oran and was held previously by the Germans. (*See map*) The Germans cleared the town out before they left. While here I made the friendship of several American rangers who fought in the invasions of Africa.   The native Arabs dressed typical Arabic style. A towel wound around their head and a sheet around their body and in most cases no shoes served as every day wear. They begged liked little kids for cigarettes and clothes. An old torn shirt or torn pair of dungarees was like giving him a new world. They would immediately put them on and strut away as if in a brand new suit. Most of them are very dirty with sores all over their feet and bodies, however the French inhabitants are much better. They dress like we do. Because of the destruction by the war the Arabs moved to loot the cities of whatever they could get. They can never be trusted. They all carried one or two knives and would not hesitate to use them. Nemours is a backward country, as most of these cities all are; they have very little machinery. Our trucks and jeeps do most of our work while burrows do work for the Arabs. The French employ them to work at the docks for a $1.00 a week. They were paid in Francs. One Franc equals two cents. One hundred Centimes makes up for one Franc. Wine is the most profitable drink which costs around 2 Francs.   Nemours is just typical African town,, small, compact, and in most cases, along the waters edge. It is a good town, but for one Liberty.

NEMOURS, AFRICA
(150 miles from Oran)

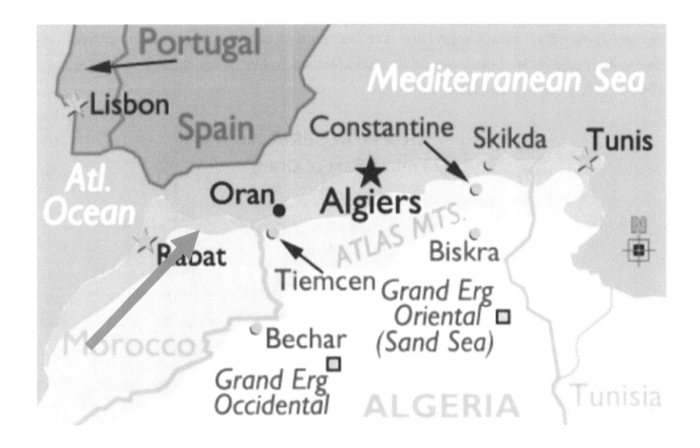

May-7-1943Friday - Nemours, Africa

We went ashore and played football and baseball. The Arabs watched us closely, probably wondering why we ran around so.

May-8-1943 Saturday - Nemours, Africa

This day was similar to the 7th.

May-9-1943 Sunday – "Mothers Day" - At Sea to Arzew

At 07.30 we got underway again. We had trouble with our 3" 50 caliber and this delayed us for a day. We sailed without a convoy. All we had was two L.C.I. (Landing Craft Infantry) as escorts. We were once more traveling East. We hugged the coast line all the way.

At 04:30 we sited a small town. It looked bigger than Nemours. This is was our destination, Arzew. I noticed our friends were here. We anchored off shore. We are getting closer every day to the battlefields. I have now at this time received news of the fall of Tunis. (*See map*) We had today our regular chicken dinner.

ARZEW, ALGERIA
(25 miles East of Oran)

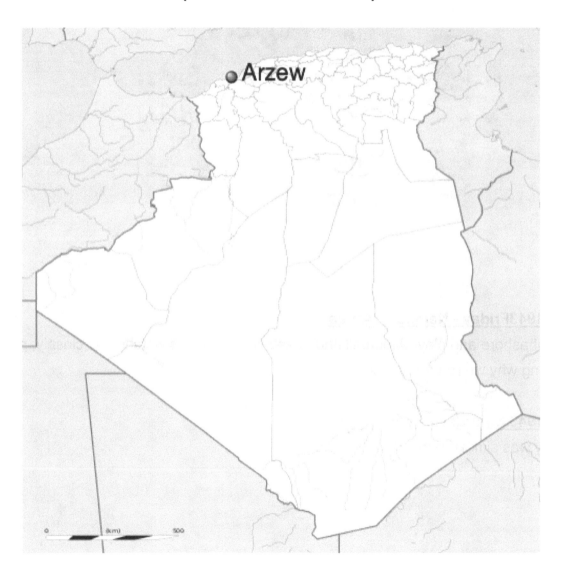

May-10-1943 Monday - Arzew, Africa

We were paid today. I drew no money.

May-11-1943 Tuesday - Arzew, Africa

I went on Liberty in Arzew with Kenny. We had a good time wandering through the small streets. We bought dates, postal cards which we could not mail, lemons as big as apples, which we used for lemonade. As we walked around among the Arabs and Frenchmen, the kids ran up to us and asked us for dates which we obligingly gave them. We had Liberty from 07.00 – 10.00. We also attended a church; which was small but neat. L. Eglise was its name. We then boarded our Liberty ship and returned to our ship.

ALGERIA

May-12-1943 Wednesday - Arzew, Africa

We tied up next to the 349, which contained some of my friends. After little work was completed to our ship, I had a long talk with my buddies; we then moved out beyond the breakwater. That night we sat on deck and watched the sunset. It is one of the most beautiful sites one can imagine, with the sun setting behind small distant mountains with sky blue water as a foreground and reddish white clouds floating in the clear blue sky. This is the best time of day.

May-13-1943 Thursday - Arzew, Africa

Today we prepared our L.C.T. (Landing Craft Tank) for launching.

May-14-1943 Friday - At Sea Sailing East

Today is one month since we left NY. It seems but a week. We launched our L.C.T. (Landing Craft Tank) with out any trouble. We listed our ship and our L.C.T. into the water. We then went back to tie up with 349 again. We are now waiting for sailing orders. They finally came at 22.00 after waiting several hours. As we sailed East again, we went on four on and four off. The water is like a sheet of glass.

May-15-1943 Saturday - At Sea

We are now passing Algiers, (*See map*). It is one of the larges cities in the N.A. (North Africa). It has many large buildings. We spotted a sub, which surfaced and recognized itself as ours.

May-16-1943 Sunday - Bougie, Africa

We spotted an enemy sub and fired upon same. It pulled out of range and escaped. Before dawn, a airplane, probably German, flew over and dropped a flair. It lit up our convoy as if it was daylight. At 08.00 we pulled into Bougie. It is the best town or city we have yet visited. It has many modern buildings. It is 150 miles from Tunis. We are the first American sailors to arrive at this port. The Germans, as they did in other previous ports, stripped it of everything, even taking clothes from the Arabs. There were several ships sunk in the harbor and many other ships were scuttled by the French while tied up at piers. In this city, eggs and potatoes are the principle foods. Champagne is the chief drink, cost 50 Francs a bottle.

LOADING L.C.T. ON L.S.T.

Bougie 5/16/43

Drawing by Al Klumpp

May-17-1943 Monday - Bougie, Africa

We started to unload our cargo. The British sailors did our work. While on watch this night II talked with members of the British Eighth Army. They had a big Nazi Flag which I tried to buy, but was unsuccessful. Their Army isn't far from us. As they advance, we follow.

May-18-1943 Tuesday - Bougie, Africa

At 01.00 I went on Liberty with Norman Kepley. We had until 22.00 to return. We were the first Americans to make Liberty. As we walked through the streets, which were very hilly, the small children ran into their homes calling "Amicanos". Their parents came to the streets and gave us a very warm welcome.   The French people are nice, but the Arabs we had to watch. They were still for the Germans. We drank wine with some Scotch Soldiers. They praised our airmen, planes, tanks and everything else made by America. They admit the Americans won the last war and we are wining this one too. Although the French people had been cleared out of almost everything, they were still willing to share what they had with us.

May-19-1943 Wednesday - Bougie, Africa

Our ship is still being unloaded. At evening we had an air alert. The next town, about 30 miles away was raided. The sky was littered up with all colored shells. It is a beautiful site to see, but sometimes not so nice to be in. Bougie was covered with a cloud of smoke within a few minutes. There is a heavy smoke which clings to the ground.

May-20-1943 Thursday - Bougie, Africa

Today I saw Bougie Ironworks. (Bougie is a Mediterranean port city on the Gulf of Béjaïa in Algeria) They have an elevated system to bring iron ore to the foundry. The mines are 14 miles away. They are located behind the mountain range. The elevated system runs through woods, over streams and roads until it reaches its destination.   Tonight we had another air raid. We could feel the bombing of the next city very well.

May-21-1943 - Bougie, Africa

Still unloading our cargo.

May-21-1943 - Bougie, Africa

We are unloading the pontoon by means of a small crane we bought with us. It is a slow job, however, we finished unloading today. We then moved out beyond the breakwater and anchored. We then opened up the bow doors and went swimming. We made a diving board and attached it to our ramps.

May 22, 23 – NO LOG Saturday – Sunday - Bougie, Africa

May-24-1943 Monday - Bougie, Africa

I went ashore and met some Limey (English) soldiers. We went to a tea garden run by some French people. While here I met some buddies from other L.S.T.'s. While in the tea garden a attractive French girl, gave me all the tea and cakes I wanted. I offered to pay her, but she refused to accepted anything. After finishing my tea the soldiers wanted me to return with them to their camp but I had to refuse their offer and return to my ship. It was unfortunate they had German and Italian souvenirs for me.   During tonight's raid a large bomber got shot down. It came straight down and fell into the ocean.

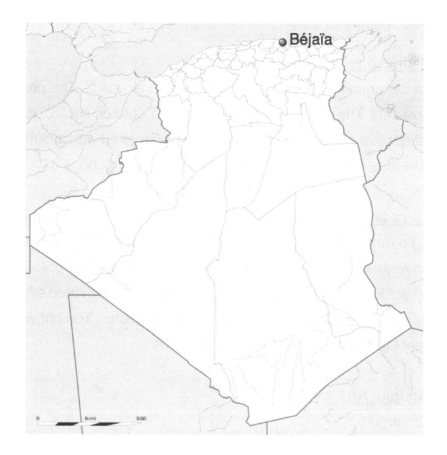

Béjaïa is a Mediterranean port city on the Gulf of Béjaïa in Algeria; it is the capital of Béjaïa Province, Kabylia It was formerly known under various European names, such as **Budschaja** in German, **Bugia** in Italian, and **Bougie** in French

16

May-26-1943 Tuesday – At Sea

Today we left Bougie and sailed once more East. Time 04.15.

May-27-1943 Wednesday - Bone, Africa

At 15.00 we arrived Bone. It is the third largest city in Tunisia. With a population of 50,000. This town has been one of the worst bombed cities in Africa. It is a P.T. base. They had a raid here a day ago and quite a lot of ships and been sunk, some completely broken in half. We proceeded in through the harbor, where some light cruisers, gun boats and all kinds of freighters were tied up. We could not find a place to tie up so we had to drop anchor outside the breakwater. We still have aboard our ship two rollers, probably for sheet metal. Each weights thirty two tons and yet we haven't been able to locate any means of taking them off. The crane here has just been bombed. After lying at anchor for several hours we received orders to move again. We then started East again, still having our rollers aboard. It seems we will never get rid of them.

May-28-1943 Friday – 11:03 - Bizerte

We are now in Bizerte. *(See map p.19)* It is only 100 some miles from Italy. On the beach we can see wrecked trucks and other vehicles. The land here is flat, more like the desert. Trees here are becoming scarce in fact it is quite barren. It is now getting dark and from beyond the mountains there is coming bombers, and escorts on their way toward Italy.

May-29-1943 Saturday – Lac-De-Bizerte

We had a peaceful night, although the Germans claimed they raided Bizerte and sunk many of our invasion ships. We are still anchored out in the Mediterranean Sea, we were suppose to pull out into the Harbor, but because of floating mines we were forced to anchor out. There are some ships now exploding the strayed mines and clearing the harbor. Some to close to our ship.

May-30-1943 Sunday – Lac-De-Bizerte

Last night we had an air raid. Dive bombers came in close and dropped their bombs. We heard one plane coming in and a bomb whistling. It was so dark we couldn't see him, he was coming in under our fire. The bomb exploded off our Starboard Beam doing no damage. The plane was then over our bow within feet. It gave our gunners very little opportunity to open fire; however they did respond, and did come close, every close. Other bombers were dropping on the beach and in other unimportant places. Shrapnel was hitting all along our deck, afterwards I swept it off and I saved a small piece for myself. My GQ (General Quarters) station is in the can. I am up high and can see everything that goes on. I man the phones that keep the officers in touch with the gunners. The officers are below me in the wheel house. I failed to mention that one of our gunners was unfortunate enough to stop a piece of shrapnel in his shoulder. It glanced of his helmet into his arm; it was fortunate it didn't hit him direct and cause more damage.

We are now going into the harbor to tie up. While passing through one ship ripped the breakwater we passed many destroyed ships, many were French. Some ships are completely sunk and we had to pass over them. While passing through, one ship ripped her bottom opened. The enemy tried and did a good job of blocking up the inlet, which is narrow. This inlet is about two miles long, then it opens up into a big bay. The city of Bizerte is built up on both sides of this channel. Every building shows signs of bombing; while some are completely leveled. While proceeding inland we saw ships that were so completely destroyed we could not identify them. They looked like a pile of scrap iron. We anchored between an airfield and an ammunition dump which had been destroyed and now is being repaired. We no sooner dropped anchor when two enemy planes flew over at a high altitude. Nothing happened.

18

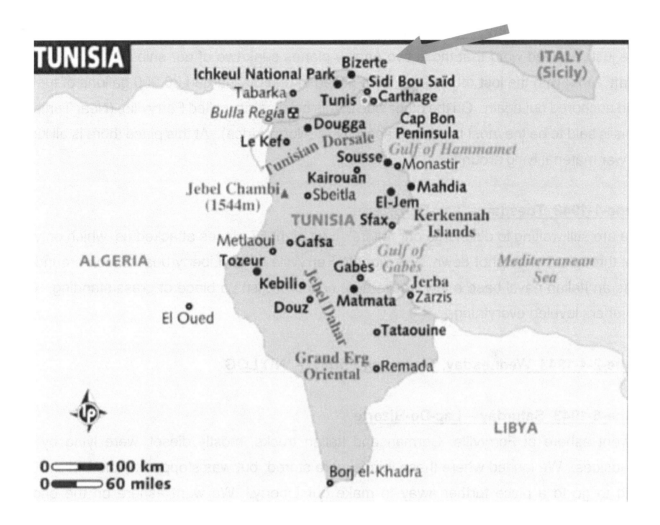

FERRYVILLE, TUNISIA

May-31-1943 Monday – Lac-De-Bizerte

We just received word that those two enemy planes sunk two of our ships, L.C.T. (Landing Craft Tank) with the lost of five lives. We pulled in and discharged 60,000 gallons of fuel oil and anchored out again. On the other side of this bay is a city called Ferryville. (Near Tunisia). This is said to be the most bombed place in N.A. (North Africa). At this place there is all kinds of war material lying around.

June-1-1943 Tuesday – Lac-De-Bizerte

We are still waiting to discharge our rollers. Last night 57 planes attacked us, which only 17 got through, 6 were shot down. We went to Ferryville in our Liberty boat to look around. It was an Italian naval base a few weeks ago, now there isn't a blade of grass standing. Our bombers leveled everything.

June-2-4-1943 Wednesday, Thursday, Friday – NO LOG

June-5-1943 Saturday – Lac-De-Bizerte

I went ashore at Ferryville. German and Italian trucks, mostly diesel, were lying by the roadsides. We landed where these things were stored, but was stopped by the British. We had to go to a place further away to make our Liberty. We went ashore on the end of Ferryville. This town was the best town yet. There were but a few Arabs. I was composed mostly of French. I met an American soldier of the Construction Engineers, who wanted to get me some German possessions, but as in Bougie had to leave before he could get them for me. Three fellows on our Liberty party failed to return so they were left there ashore all night and picked up in the morning. They were then restricted to our ship.

June-7-1943 Monday – Lac-De-Bizerte

I spent most of today acting as engineer for our Liberty boat with Garcia as operator. We did errands for the officers taking Liberty parties ashore.

June-8-1943 Tuesday – Lac-De-Bizerte

Today things began to happen. We got four more Higgins boats to compete a group of six. (A Higgins boat is a landing craft used extensively in amphibious landings in World War II; designed by Andrew Higgins). A group of soldiers also came aboard, about two hundred of the Fifteenth Commando Division. We then practiced launching the small crafts from our ship. These soldiers expected to return to the States, but now they know they have another job to do. Our L.S.T. was one of the first to move into Bizerte, the rest are slowly coming in. Invasion doesn't seem to be far off now.

June-9-1943 Wednesday – Lac-De-Bizerte

We are still making practice landings. All we do is launch them into the water, the rest is up to them. I talked with an American Commando today who was in Tunis when it fell. He told me the prisoners came in all night, all the next day and all that night, 360,000 in all. The enemy drove their own trucks into camp. They were singing and laughing, they told the Americans that they didn't want to fight no more then we did. As it gets dark our planes leave and later during the night we can see flashes of light from our bombs.   This keeps up for hours.

June-10-1943 Thursday – Lac-De-Bizerte

At 06.00 we got underway. We headed toward Tunis. At a given point we started our "invasion". We had seven other L.S.T.(Landing, Ship Tank) for vessels created during World War II to support amphibious operations by carrying vehicles, cargo, and etc.) and some L.C.I. (Landing Craft Infantry) for escorts. The soldiers proceeded inland and "captured" their objective.

June-11-1943 Friday – Lac-De-Bizerte

We went on maneuvers similar to those of yesterday. After discharging the soldiers, we proceeded back, while the soldiers walked back,   sometimes as many as twenty miles. They lived off of field rations, which is nothing more than dog biscuits and canned stew.

June-12-1943 Saturday – Lac-De-Bizerte

Our ship was named Flag Ship today. We now have control of the other ships in our group. We started on maneuvers today; but had to return because of a sub warning. We then practiced landing in the bay.   Last night about eleven o'clock we saw about hundred and fifty forts fly over (see next page). Later that night we received word that, Pantelleria surrendered to us. (*See map p.23*) (It is an island in the Strait of Sicily; SW of Sicily and E. of Tunisian) We had all plans of invading this island. Tonight, an hour before sunset, three enemy plans flew over. They were very high,, probably just taking pictures of our base. The axis keep checking on us to find out when the invasion is coming. Our shore batteries opened fire. They then pulled out to sea and were gone.

Fort Aircraft

The Fleet Model 60K Fort was the only aircraft designed and built by Canadians during the Second World War and was also the first all-metal monoplane built by Fleet Aircraft of Canada (Fort Erie).

Wikipedia

June-13-1943 Sunday – Lac-De-Bizerte

Practice landings were going on today as usual.

We fed the Army a chicken dinner. It was the first "meal" in many months. They never stopped talking about this meal and the fact at sitting at a table.

Today the P.38's were flying about.

June-14-1943 Monday – Lac-De-Bizerte

We weighed anchor this morning and tied up directly in front of the hangers. They are less than a block away. Their most common planes are the P40's and the P38's. We are to remove rollers.

June-15-1943 Tuesday – Lac-De-Bizerte

I received mail today. It was the Lawndale Press and the Suburban Times. I also received some handkerchiefs' from Thelm. The weather is very warm.

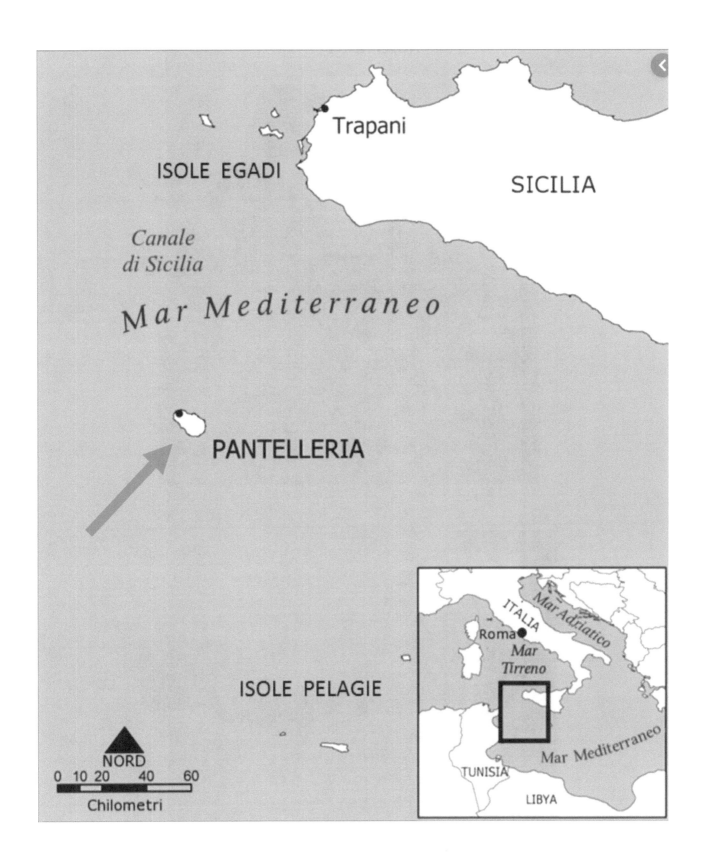

June-16-1943 Wednesday – Lac-De-Bizerte

Today I received welcome mail from my family and Thelm. After reading my mail I took a walk around Bizerte. I first went through the once held German and Italian hangers. Most of the hangers are now empty. Several hangers have many French planes that were completely destroyed by our bombs. Because of the speed that our Army traveled, one hanger was left with parts of the planes that are brand new and haven't even been uncrated. I walked through some graveyards filled with German trucks and planes, but was unable to obtain anything of importance.

June-17-1943 Thursday – Lac-De-Bizerte

It is now 05.00 and we are finally getting our rollers removed. It is a hard job with the machines they are using. It will take sometime to remove them. The other ships are loading their equipment aboard.

June-18-1943 Lac-De-Bizerte

Today we removed our rollers. We now have an empty ship

June-19-1943 Lac-De-Bizerte

We all turned to and cleaned up our ship for our cargo.

June-20-1943 Father's Day – Lac-De-Bizerte

We talked with fellows on the P.T. boat tied next to us. It was later taken ashore for repair. They were patrolling off the coast of Italy where they were raided. They made a dash, but a bomb came close and blew off a propeller. They did, however, managed to return to their base.

June-21-1943 Monday – Lac-De-Bizerte

Today we loaded our ship with Army trucks and jeeps all containing explosives. Several trucks are carrying land mines. In the afternoon we practiced abandoning ship and fire drills. We now have about 175 soldiers aboard.

June-22-1943 Lac-De-Bizerte

Today Harry Johnson and myself did the crews wash. It took us all day. At 10.30 we had an air raid, one at 03.30, one at 04.50 and one at 07.00. This was unusual to have so many in one night. The axis must be worried because of the frequent visits of their scout planes.

June-23-1943 Wednesday – Lac-De-Bizerte

We just had two more air raids. At 5.00 our small boats brought the rest of our soldiers aboard. We now have four hundred or better. They are stripped down to as little as possible to live on. We gave them our hammocks to sleep on. They are going to sleep on the top deck. They are having one time trying to stay in them.

June-24-1943 Thursday – Lac-De-Bizerte

At two o'clock we got underway. All ships except tankers and some tenders, left the bay. We are now in position and are anchored outside of Bizerte. The question now is whether or not we are going to invade now. It might only be a dry run.

June 25-1943 Friday – Lac-De-Bizerte

We found out at 24.00 that is was only a dry run. We anchored in a bay near Tunis *(see map)* and discharged our troops. They came aboard shortly after their and embarkment. We then laid at anchor for the rest of the night. We have a constant parole of P40's and Spitfires flying over us. They are attempting to keep this movement as much a secret as possible. At 08.30 we have gotten underway once more. Flotilla of about two hundred ships is moving back towards Bizerte. At one o'clock we joined with another convoy consisting of transports, tankers, one battlewagon, cruiser and several destroyers.   Just awhile back we sited another convoy. We gather together just outside of Bizerte and dropped anchor where we sat until the next day.

June-26-1943 Saturday – Lac-De-Bizerte

Today we moved once again, into Bizerte Bay. While pulling in we saw a convoy that was countless. It extended from one end of the horizon to the other end. It was moving toward Tunis. We still have our equipment aboard; but the soldiers, driver and infantry, have gone ashore. The moon is in its last quarter. We are probably waiting for the moon to disappear completely. Today I received twenty-seven letters. It was a pleasure to receive so much mail after having so little news from home. Three more destroyers have just pulled in the mist of us. We are getting over anxious for the big movement. From the soldiers it is rumored we will invade on July the 4th, after which we are expecting to return to the States. We had little air activity in the last two days, probably because of our increase in our own air patrols. We had 2 more air raids during the night. No planes were sighted.

June-27-1943 Sunday – Lac-De-Bizerte

We are still waiting for the return of the soldiers. We have just our crew aboard now. During the stay of the soldiers we ate the same as they, field rations, mostly stew and biscuits. Everyday is about the same, warm and sunny, with swimming off our ramp.

Today warnings were posted to the effect of not entering the Chartroom. The Captain has received sealed orders and has his charts lined out. We have reason to believe that we will land in Italy itself. The moon is slowly disappearing, bringing the final hour closer.

June-28-1943 Monday – Lac-De-Bizerte

At 03.30 we had a air raid alert. No planes were sighted. We are still anchored in the same place as yesterday, still waiting the return of our soldiers. The Captain stated today he will tell us when we sail, where and when we will invade. This will be the first act of this kind aboard our ship. All other runs have been kept from us as much as possible. At 11.03 today it has been one month since we have dropped anchor in Bizerte. Time has actually flew by; probably because of the numerous air raids.

June-29-1943 Tuesday – Lac-De-Bizerte

Last night was very quite. Our Captain was ashore with other L.S.T's officers and Army officers. They were in conference with the Admiral. On his return, which was at 11.30 and during an air alert, our health records and pay accounts were gotten in order to be taken ashore for safe keepings. I was issued a Thompson Machine Gun. *(see picture)* This is to assist me in my rounds of the ship. It is to protect our ship from Arabs who might try and destroy it. It has been done by placing a mine on the side. The Arabs are very easy to bride and this sort of thing occurs once in a while, even though our ships help a lookout for such actions.

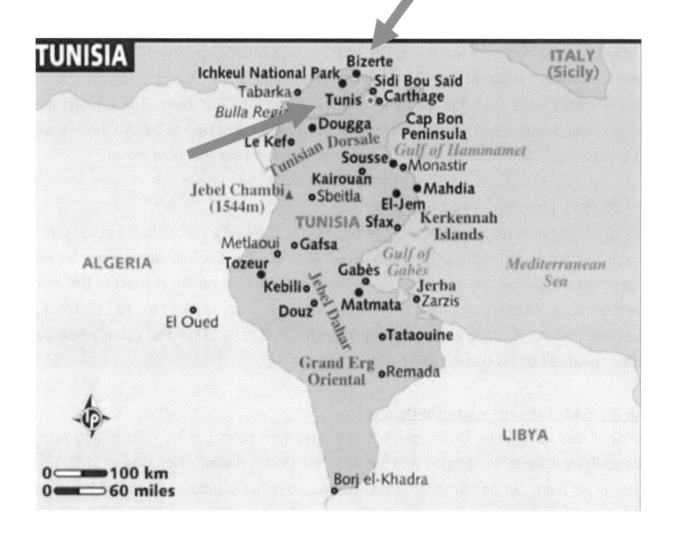

June-30-1943 Wednesday – Lac-De-Bizerte

At 16.15 we had a air alert that lasted only 5 minutes. We are not having trouble with our mail. Mr. Myers has taken over Mr. Browning's job of censoring and has so far done not a very good job. I found most of my letter that I written to Dad, in an ash can. It should have been returned even though it was censored. I don't know how long this has been going on, so I don't know how many letters did go through.

July-1-1943 Thursday – Lac-De-Bizerte

Last night was very calm with no alerts. Today we had our regular swimming party. All we do is open up our bow and in we go. We have a little homemade boat named Marie, in which we have lots of fun. During our swimming we had a practice drill of unloading wounded patients from Higgins Boats into our L.S.T. We did this by lowering our ramp and lowering the ramp of the Higgins and running it up our ramp. After unloaded the Higgins backed down and another one came in. It is an ideal way of collecting the wounded. We received orders that from the July the 5th on, we will wear shirts and life belts and good shoes at all times. Probably we will get underway at this time. This afternoon more ships pulled into Lac-De-Bizerte. They were American ships. Five destroyers anchored near us. Four battleships are out at the breakwater and another is coming into anchor. The famous light cruiser Boise is in Bougie.

July-2-1943 Friday – Lac-De-Bizerte

Last night was another calm night with no air alerts. During the day very little happened except for a G.Q. (General Quarters) at 17.30 with no planes sighted. We just received word that the Germans expect us to invade on the third; as yet we still haven't been told when or where.

July-3-1943 Saturday – Lac-De-Bizerte

Last night was also calm. In the morning from 08.00 to 12.00 I was on watch of which most of the time I spent on the can helping to receive signals and taking positions of the other ships. At 09.30 we had an air raid alert with no planes sighted. At 12.00 we had another alert and sighted seventeen planes, probably ours for no activity took place. In the afternoon we went swimming. We also did some diving off the side of the ship.

THOMPSON SUBMACHINE GUN

Thompson Submachine Gun, Caliber .45

M1921 Thompson with vertical fore-grip and 100 round
Type 'C' drum magazine

The **Thompson submachine gun** is an American submachine gun invented by John T. Thompson in 1918 which became infamous during the Prohibition era, being a signature weapon of various organized crime syndicates in the United States. It was a common sight in the media of the time, being used by both law enforcement officers and criminals. The Thompson submachine gun was also known informally as the **"Tommy Gun"**, **"Tôm Sông"**, **"Annihilator"**, **"Chicago Typewriter"**, **"Chicago Submachine"**, **"Chicago Piano"**, **"Chicago Style"**, **"Chicago Organ Grinder"**, **"Drum Gun"**, **"The Chopper"**, and simply **"The Thompson"**.

The Thompson was favored by soldiers, criminals, police, FBI, and civilians alike for its large .45 ACP cartridge and high volume of fully automatic fire. It has since gained popularity among civilian collectors for its historical significance. It has considerable significance in popular culture, especially in works about the Prohibition era and World War II, and is among the best-known firearms in history. The original fully automatic Thompsons are no longer produced, but numerous semi-automatic civilian versions are still being manufactured by Auto-Ordnance. These retain a similar appearance to the original models, but they have various modifications in order to comply with US firearm laws.

Wikipedia

LICATA, SICILY

July-4-1943 Sunday – Lac-De-Bizerte

After I completed a 24.00 to 08.00 we got underway at 07.00. We had revelry 05.30 and then manned our special sea stations. All we did is move across the lake to the far end. We are going to practice with pontoons. We have these pontoons along both sides of our ship. When our ship is beached the pontoons form a bridge from our ramps to the shore. We then started to beach our ship. When we came in to a close distance to the shore we dropped our stern anchor which is used to pull us off when our beaching maneuvers is finished, it was dropped out too far and before we ran on to the beach our cable ran out. It isn't fastened because such an accident may happen and a sudden stop would pull our fantail apart. Then we lost the whole works. We now have no anchor to pull us off the beach, which we couldn't help running onto, but fortunately we hadn't run a ground far and we emptied our ballasts tanker and back into the bay. In the meantime, our Executive Officer asked me and two other fellows to dive for our lost anchor. Our anchor had a buoy on it so we knew where it was. All we had to do was to dive and fasten the line to the anchor. We then went out in a Higgins Boat and anchored next to our lost anchor. Mr. Browning, a very good swimmer was also along. We all dove in and tried our best to descend to the bottom; but was unable to reach it due to the great pressure. It was thirty foot deep. Too much for any of us. The line from the anchor broke. We then had just approximate idea where it was.

We then tried diving head gear, but still were unsuccessful. While waiting for the other ships, who were graveling to make progress, we went swimming. I ran into a large jelly fish and was stung by it, creating a rash which didn't amount to anything, except a burning sensation. The other ship finally picked up our lost cable and got it aboard. We spent all afternoon doing this operation, which was a lot of fun and a lot of work. It is now 20.00 and we are still pulling in our anchor. Next, our bow anchor which broke and had to be pulled up by hand. This is quite a task, fortunately I was diving while this was going on. This operation was finished about 21.00. We then had our stern anchor in control and we then moved out into the center of the lake where we anchored by our stern anchor. What helped us to hold us back was the weather; it is very hot during the day.

July-5-1943 Monday – Lac-De-Bizerte

Although there was a slight moon, there was not air alert. We had revelry at 05.00. We got underway at 05.30 proceeding to the docks in front of the hangers. We tied up and directly afterword the 350, with Herby Hansen aboard tied up to us on our Starboard side. Then the 349 tied up to our portside. We immediately began to load on the rest of our Army trucks and supplies. It is now 10.30 and we are almost finished our loading. We have taken on many guns, 40mm, 50cal. We now have a total of forty-nine guns. At 14.30 we sited enemy planes, high overhead. The shore batteries opened fire and drove them out of range. After chow, the Army Cornel told us we were going to invade Sicily. He told us this was the key point of the war. We have everything that is in North Africa behind us and if we fail the enemy will then attack us. We have the best coastal gunners in Africa on board our ship.   An LST tied up to the 350 which has a runway for the two small Piper Cubs. They are going to be used for scouting and in their hull is mules, to be set free and run ashore and set of the land mines and traps, thus saving a lot of lives.   It is now 21.00 and we are leaving our present position and heading in toward the center of the bay. We will now wait for order to invade. We are now dropping our stern anchor. It is 22.30.

July-6-1943 Tuesday – Lac-De-Bizerte

At 04.00 we had a red alert. Enemy bombers flew over us and dropped flairs. They dropped during the entire raid a total of twenty-five flares. They light the whole lake up. They dropped quite a few bombs. They flew over and over. Our search lights played all over the sky. They picked up the plane directly overhead. We opened fire with the shore batteries. One or maybe more shells hit it square in the center. Smoke immediately came into view and the plane went into a tailspin. It hit the ground with a great explosion. Flames shot many feet into the air while our guns trained on another. We brought down three more in this manner. Any others brought down, we as yet have no official info.

It is a beautiful sight to see all the traces of various colors reaching out into the darkness and bring down enemy planes; but it isn't so pleasant when they dive at us and we can't see them. After these planes were brought down three green flares were dropping and the enemy planes took off and left. This raid lasted over an hour. It is now 13.00 and the sun is 107 in the shade. The decks are so hot we can't stand on them.

We just looked at the map of Italy and saw where we are going to land. It's location on the south side of Sicily. There is to be 2,000,000 men to invade at different points.

At that particular point we are going to invade. There are five pill boxes and behind them are the heavy guns. Three Cruisers are now anchored in the bay. It is also reported that three carriers are lying out beyond the breakwater. We were told that our mail is being held in Africa until after the invasion.

At sundown a terrific wind arose. It was a relief but is was also a menace to our ships. Because our Bow Anchor is broke, we anchor from the stern. At 22.00 our ship broke loose and headed for the ship directly in front of us. Everyone was in turmoil. We got our engines running just in time. In the meantime, our stern anchor caught. This saved our ship as well as the others. Our ship swung within 10 feet from the other ships. This incident almost put us out of the invasion. We then pulled into position again and dropped our bow anchor. It was then 24.00 time to go off watch.

July-7-1943 Wednesday – Lac-De-Bizerte

Because of our results in the last air raid and of the high wind we had no air alerts last night. At 11.00 the six boats came along side with the infantry. We are now fully loaded with over two hundred soldiers. The soldiers are now studying maps which they have placed on the deck of the Locato. They show the streets and every valuable information that will assist them. We have the best armed ship, with the best shots in Africa with us. At 11.00 we started to pull up the Bow Anchor. This is a tiresome job. It has pulled in, in six ft. sections. We are, as far as we know, going to sail with no Bow Anchor. It is now 12.00 and we are getting underway. We are pulling out of Lac- De-Bizerte. All the other LST's are following. We have now dropped anchor outside the breakwater. The time is 14.00. All the other ships, cruisers, destroyers etc., have also pulled anchor and left. We were told we will strike Saturday morning at 03.00, six hours after the first wave of soldiers land. We are on condition two, probably we will stay on this until after the evasion. All we do now is wait. Our captain just gave us a few pointers on what we are going to do. We are the guide ship, of all the rest. We are to leave Birzerte at 05.00 and sail East. We will sail toward Malta *(see map)* where we will all unite, that is all that is going to take the "yellow beach" and then proceed toward Sicily. We shall discharge our troops and equipment and then pull out to sea and drop anchor. We then will be a hospital ship.

July-8-1943 Thursday – At Sea

We are now pulling anchor at 04.45. We are forming into a convoy of many ships and proceeding East along the mainland. Another group of ships are now joining us from the West. They are mostly, cruisers, destroyers, and troop transports. They are not waiting for us, they are moving ahead of us. It is now 16.15 and I just came off my four hour watch. Nothing happened on my watch except for a group of fighters, about twenty-five, flying over toward Sicily. We were told that our ship will be one of the two that is to be beached and our skipper said we will beach it at any cost. We, the Americans, are attacking from the West and South while the English are attacking from the East. Although we have a countless number of ships, we are told that it is but a small group that is going over. At 16.00 we passed Pantelleria, we will not proceed South until parallel with Malta, then we will cross over and meet another force probably the one that passed us this morning, then we will proceed North to Sicily and start our invasion.

This has been the chance we have all be waiting for and we are all eager to put this over to the best of our ability. It is now 20.00 and I am coming off watch again. We are now parallel with Malta and have changed our direction toward Malta. We are leaving Africa in the background. We now have thirty hours to go. We are having nice weather. It is very warm and the water is very calm.

July-9-1943 Friday – At Sea

The wind was blowing up and the sea is getting very rough. Our ship is taking the worst beating it was ever given. We passed Malta at 15.00. It was bending in every direction. One of our forward boats got loose and caused quite a commotion. It banged against the davit so hard that when it came time to use it, it was complete out of commission. After securing the boat we had a G.Q. this was a 23.30. I immediately took my station with the can where I remain until 05.40 the next evening. A half moon was still shining, which sets about 01.30, when we came into view of Sicily. Our planes had done their job by dropping bombs and strafing the streets of various cities we were told to invade.

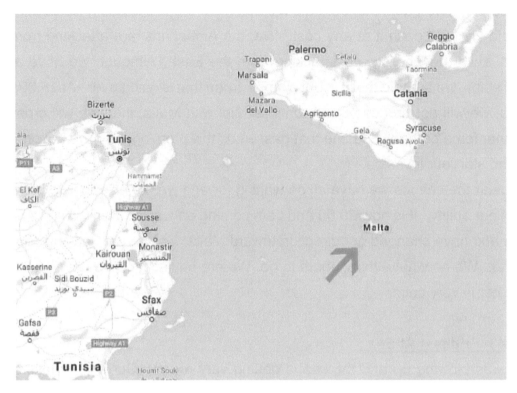

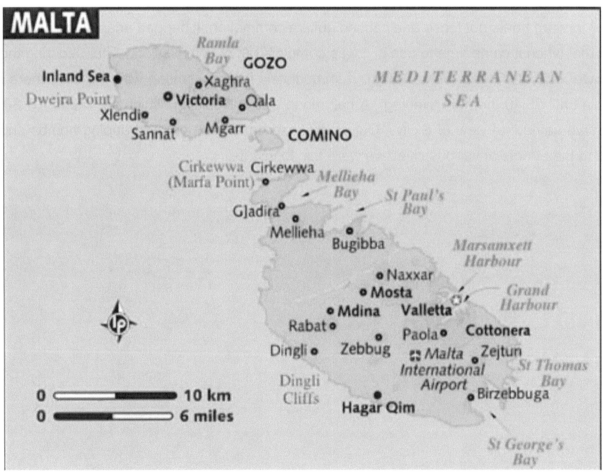

July-10-1943 Saturday – Lac-De-Bizerte

We pulled close to Sicily on the moon set and dropped anchor within one mile from the shore. We were supposed to be three and a half miles from shore. As soon as the anchor dropped a German plane whipped directly over us. He was going so fast he probably didn't' see us. Our small boats then left for shore, this was at 03.00.   The cruisers put their lights on a destroyer to draw the enemies fire. It so happened that because we were out of positions we were also in the path of the search lights and fire. Our anchor engine was broke thus making our anchor a set back to us. The cruisers and destroyers opened fire on the shore batteries. We were between our ships and the shore. This all happened between three o'clock and daybreak. Dawn was braking when the enemy got our position. We immediately opened up our engines and maneuvered as best as we could with the anchors still holding us. The shells were dropping where our bow was and also dropping in our wake. We cut our chain with a torch and maneuvered out further. By this time small boats had discharged their troops and returned. Some small boats were riddled with machine gun fire, fortunately they all returned. The sun is now up and we could see where we were. There was still a little shore action going on, this was at 12.00.

A ME109 came down the beach strafing and dropping bombs. We opened fired and nipped him. He flew along the beach and then into a house. There was a explosion, then fire appeared. The house burned to the ground. this was easy pickens for our cruisers and destroyers. While the cruisers stayed out of range and fired of the shore batteries and fired the destroyers came in close and fired shell after shell until the enemy position fell. A tank position which we could see through the glasses was destroyed by a battle wagon. While this was going on enemy planes were flying about. Because firing at night would have given our position away we had today sit tight and wait until daybreak, then we opened up. The beach heads were well established by 10.00. Until 12.00 we did nothing but maneuver; then we were given orders and went in and beached our ship. Although we had supremacy of the air we had to man our battle stations continually, because enemy planes would sneak in from over the hills and catch us napping. We then unloaded our equipment as fast as we could my means of a pontoon bride. While unloading enemy planes would sneak in and drop bombs and strafe the beaches. At 16.00 we finished unloading and took on some wounded men, four Italians and five Americans. We then pulled out of the beach and maneuvered out to where we were before. We maneuvered for several hours, after which we met three other L.S.T.'s, an LCI's and three sub chasers. (Submarine chaser; see article). Two cruisers and several destroyers escorted us out to sea then left us.

July-11-1943 Sunday – at Sea

We are still on are way back to Bizerte. At 12.30 we sighted Pantelleria. We sighted Africa at 15.00. We then followed the African coast until we reached Bizerte. We dropped anchor out beyond the beach water at 01.30, Monday Morning. We stayed here all night.

July-12-1943 Monday – Lac-De-Bizerte

At 09.00 we pulled anchor and sailed into Bizerte Harbor where we tied up in front of the airport again. We discharged our wounded and began cleaning our ship. At 13.00 we began loading our ship again, so as we can return to Sicily as fast as possible. Harry Johnson and myself are doing the wash for the fellows while the ship is being loaded. It is now 17.00 and we are all loaded. We have many jeeps, half trucks and other motorized equipment. There is, like last time, over five hundred soldiers.

While we were on the invasion the enemy came over Bizerte and tried to knock out our piers. Out of fourteen planes six were shot down. They did drop quite a few bombs. Many of these bombs are still dangerous, for they have not gone off. These areas are blocked off. At 17.30 we had an air alert and another 18.45. The L.S.T. next to us has just loaded up with three hundred Arabian. The Arabs that ride them are from French Morocco and are very highly feared by the Germans. They do mostly sneer work and very good at it. They wear robes over their uniforms. They form a picturesque scene while riding toward our ships. They are exactly in appearance as they are shown in motion pictures.

July-13-1943 Tuesday – Lac-De-Bizerte

We had no air alerts during the night. We are still tied up in front of the hangers although we have been completely loaded since yesterday. During the night we had our anchor hoist fixed. At 11.30 we went into position outside of Bizerte and started toward Sicily once again. Moroccans faced East and prayed. At 15.00 we passed Tunis. The weather was great, it is cold and the water is mild. At 19.00 a large convoy passes us coming probably from Sicily. At 24.00 when I was going on watch we were maneuvering for subs. It was a beautiful night with the calm water and large bright moon shinning.

SUBMARINE CHASER

USS *PC-815*, a US subchaser that served in World War II

U.S. Navy **submarine** chasers were designed specifically to destroy **German** submarines in **World War I**, and **Japanese** and **German** submarines in **World War II**. The small 110-foot (34 m) **SC-1-class submarine chasers** of the design used in World War I carried the hull designator **SC** (for **S**ubmarine **C**haser).[1] Their main weapon was the **depth charge**. They also carried **machine guns** and **anti-aircraft guns**. The similar-sized **SC-497-class** was built for World War II. Also in World War II, larger 173-foot (53 m) **PC-461-class submarine chasers** used the **PC** hull classification symbol (for **P**atrol, **C**oastal).

In early 1915, the British Admiralty selected the US Elco company for the production of 50 Motor Launches for anti-submarine work, British industry being at maximum capacity. This order was eventually increased by a further 530. The whole order was completed by November 1916, and the vessels entered Royal Navy service. The vessels were 80 feet (24 m) in length and capable of 20 knots (37 km/h). They were armed with a 3-pounder gun, towed paravanes to attack submarines and, later, depth charges. Additional motor launches of the Fairmile A and B and other classes were built for World War II.

War service

The British sub chasers were operated around the coast in defence. However, they were uncomfortable, wet and not suited to British sea conditions. Although used during the First World War, they were sold when the war ended.

Submarine chasers were used mostly by the United States Coast Guard in World War II for destroying German U-boats that were stationed off the coast of the United States that were trying to sink merchant convoys as they departed American ports. By the end of World War II, submarine chasers had sunk around 67 German U-boats. In the Pacific Theatre, submarine chasers were used for amphibious landings, courier and escort duty.

Eight British Fairmile B Motor Launches were transferred from Canada to the US in World War II, and included the SC-1466 class of sub-chasers.

The Imperial Japanese Navy had around 250 submarine chasers in World War II, principally about 200 of the No.1-class auxiliary submarine chasers. Some of these survived to serve in the Japan Maritime Self Defense Force (JMSDF) after the war.

During Project Hula, the United States secretly transferred 32 U.S. Navy submarine chasers to the Soviet Union between 26 May and 2 September 1945, and some of these saw action in the Soviet Navy during Soviet military operations against the Japanese between 9 August and 2 September 1945. The transfer of 24 more was canceled when transfers halted on 5 September 1945, three days after the Japanese surrender. Between 1954 and 1960 all 32 transferred submarine chasers were scrapped by the Soviet Union or destroyed off its coast by mutual agreement between the two countries.

Post-war

In the decade immediately after World War II, the Soviet Union built 227 Kronshtadt-class submarine chasers, some of which remained in active service until the 1990s. Rapid developments in submarine technologies since World War II mean that submarine chasers are now obsolete, having been replaced by corvettes, frigates, and destroyers.

Survivor

The only remaining submarine chaser with intact World War II armament is the Royal Norwegian Navy's HNoMS *Hitra*, which is a touring museum today. A World War II type submarine chaser built in 1953, originally *PC1610*, is being restored in the Netherlands as *Le Fougueux*.

Wikipedia

July-14-1943 Wednesday - Licata

08.00, we are again on watch and the weather is the same. At 11.00 we sighted Sicily again. The time we reached the Harbor of Licata (see map) it was three o'clock. We immediately tied up to a pier and start dispose of our cargo. We are within a city block of the city itself. This city is also built on the side of a mountain. We could plainly see where our ships had shelled the coast. Although we have supremacy of the air, the enemy does a lot of damage at night. We are hoping to empty our ship and take on wounded prisoners and sail before dark to avoid any unnecessary bombing. It is now 17.25 and we have taken aboard our wounded, seven in all. One is a pilot who was shot down in a P-38. He is just scratched. Another is a very young German. While an American soldier was going ashore he stopped me and asked me to buy his German rifle. I agreed and therefore obtained my first real German prize. While we were tied up, one after another, DC-3's Douglas Transports landed in the nearby field. There must have been fifteen.

At 19.00 we moved out into the distance of Licata. We are waiting for two more L.S.T.'s to join us. We lost an L.S.T. on the beach. 158 had three bombs dropped in its middle and blew it to nothing. We formed our convoy at 23.00 and once again sailed to Bizerti. It is taking us about 23 hours to make our trips.

July-15-1943 Thursday- Lac-De-Bizerte

At 0.600 we pass another group of L.S.T. 's heading toward Sicily. At 15.00 we cited the coast of Africa. At dark, 23.00, we anchored outside of Bizerti.

July 16, 1943 Friday - Lac-De-Bizerte

In the morning at 0.700 we lifted anchor and started into Lac-De-Bizerte. While maneuvering between the sunken ships, we drifted into the side of the channel. Our Starboard engine had to be shut off because our "prop" were damaged, thus causing a vibration. We also stripped a hole in the bottom of the ship. We moved in with one prop and tied up at the pier in front of the hangers. Our men and trucks were waiting to enter our ships, but they were told to wait to see if our ships could make its trip to Sicily. It is now 21.00 and no loading has taken place.

Licata Harbor, Sicily

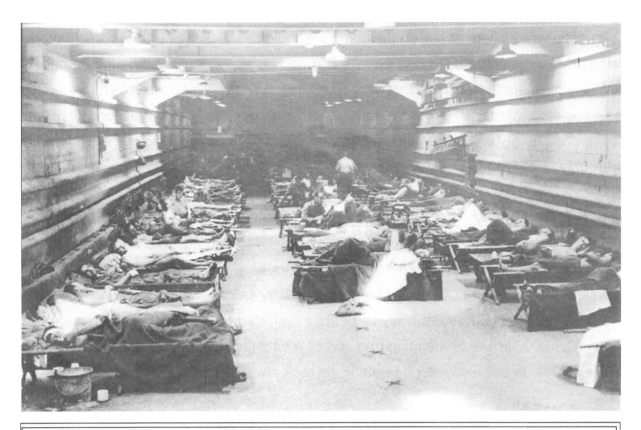

LST's Return from a Landing.
Its Empty Tank Deck Became a Hospital for Wounded Marines,

July-17-1943 Saturday – Lac-De-Bizerte

At 0.100 we left the docks and anchored in the bay. All the other L.S.T.'s are loaded, we are not. At 0.700 the L.S.T.'s made there way toward the sea. Because of our broken screw we cannot make this trip, which would have been our last one. At 0.900 we tied up at the repair pier to have our screw fixed. A diver worked on our ship all day.

July-18-1943 Sunday – Lac-De-Bizerte

Last night was quiet with no air alerts.   We probably will have very few air raids now. While our ship was being fixed Erhardt and myself got permission to leave the ship. We traveled to the different post offices to get some v-mail. We then went to a garage were Erhardt new a fellow. We then got a German truck and went riding. We needed German ammunition for our guns, so he suggested to take us to the ammunition dump. We rode through several small towns, then through Bizerte.   After going through Bizerte we headed toward the Mountain Ridge. It was rough riding for every twenty feet or so, there was a bomb creator. Someone had to go around and others were filled in. When we arrived at the dump we found that someone else had beaten us to the ammunition. We could have gone to another dump,

but our time was limited. While on the dump we could overlook the surrounding countryside.
We could see the entrance to lake Lac De Bizerte and all the towns bordering on this great
lake. We then started back on that very rough riding road. When we return to the ship, it
was completed with its new prop. We took a trial run around the "lake". We found it shimmied.
We then tied up at 19:00 and waited for further orders. We did not load our ship because of
our trouble.

July-19-1943 Monday – Lac-De-Bizerte

At 0:700 we got underway once more with the Navy LT. on board. We went out in the lake,
to test our ship again. It was decided that we could make another trip although our ship shook
from stern to bow. At 13.00 the Seabees (is the Navy's Construction Battalion. First known
as C'B's, later changed by the Navy to Seabees) started to load our ship with supplies for
Sicily. At 16:00 we went swimming and sort of a vacation ground. It has floats with diving
boards of various heights. After swimming we took a walk through the many hangers.

FORWARD GUNS

July-20-1943 Tuesday – Lac-De-Bizerte

This morning an L.S.T. brought in about two thousand prisoners. They were lined up in front of our ship and then marched away. We are still loading our ship. The cargo consists of gasoline, diesel oil, on the top side and ammunition in the hull. It is taking us several days to load because of the many small boxes. Today three Army nurses came aboard our ship, just to look around. While swimming around our ship I swam to the L.S.T. 387 and look it over. That was the one that was torpedoed while traveling to Bizerte from Oran. The whole stern (back or aft of the ship) was blown off, throwing the 3" on the con.

July-21-1943 Wednesday – Lac-De-Bizerte

We finished loading last night, but waited until 0:700 today to pull out. We anchored Lac-De-Bizerte. At 15.00 we lifted anchor and start on our way toward Sicily. We have about twelve L.S.T.'s with us. The rest were laying idol outside the breakwater. Our screw is still giving us trouble. At 19.00 we left the coast of Africa and headed East.   At 20.00 we approached Zembra, an island with high straight cliffs. We also past a convoy of cargo ships returning from Sicily. At 03.30 we were passing Pantelleria. At 17.00 we sighted Sicily.

We anchored at 18.00 outside Licata again. We shall wait until we received word to pull in and tie up. At 20.00 we tied up and began to unload. There were countless numbers of prisoners on the dock in front of our ship. They seemed anxious to board our ship and return to Africa. All they had fear in war of subs in the Mediterranean Sea.

July-22-1943 Thursday – Lacata

The ship is still being unloaded. We are still on condition two, with four on and four off.

July-23-1943 Friday – Lacata

Today thousands of prisoners were lined up on the docks and then loaded on L.S.T.'S. We are still unloading our cargo.

July-24-1943 Saturday – At Sea

At 24.30 we had an air alert. Nothing happened. At 04.30 the ammunition dump at the end of the dock caught fire. It lit the next dump too. The light from these dumps light up the city of Licata and all its surroundings, making it very dangerous for us if attacked by enemy planes. The fire burned and shells flew until we lifted anchor and got underway; which was at 0:900. All we had was a S-6 (reconnaissance night bomber). We are traveling NW to Port Empedocle. (a town in Italy on the coast of the Strait of Sicily).   Where we shall discharge the rest of our cargo. At 16.00 we sighted the Port Empedocle. (*see map*). It is divided into two sections. The city itself sits high up on a mountain. We pulled into a dock by the industrial section. It is a sulfur mining district. We had to make three (3) attempts to dock because of shelling our ships gave out. The city itself isn't very pleasant to look at. The houses are very close together and very frail looking. We are about ten miles from the fighting. The city is full of lice. Everyone has a gun on shore because of some snipers still hanging around. There seems to be very little equipment around here. There is one Liberty ship beside our ship. It is now 21.00 we are all squared away.

July-25-1943 Sunday – EMPEDOCLE
Last night forty snipers were caught. Because of lack of equipment, unloading is a long job. We brought enemy officers aboard, one of which was an Italian Admiral, the others, a General, and a Colonel.

July-26-1943 Monday – EMPEDOCLE
From the hills that over look us we hear machine gun fire and rifle fire continuously from snipers. At 20.00 the beach battalion came aboard three hundred in all. We had an hour air alert at 21.00 which didn't amount to anything.

July-27-1943 Tuesday – EMPEDOCLE
We finished unloading Seabees and loading the beach battalion by 11.00. At 13.30 we got under way all we have is a SC for an escort. We ran into some rough weather just as we left. At 16.00 we were allowed to test our guns. We threw targets in the water and fired away for about an hour. At 20.00 we sailed into Licata and dropped anchor. At 23.00 enemy planes attacked an allie airport just over the hills. They flew over our ship, but because of the darkness they didn't spot us. This raid ended at 24.30.

July-28-1943 Wednesday – Lacata
We are still anchored outside of Licata waiting for further sailing orders. Today we had our first rain fall since we came to Africa.

Porto
Empedocle

Porto Empedocle (Sicilian: *Marina*) is a town and <u>comune</u> in Italy on the coast of the **Strait of Sicily**, administratively part of the **province of Agrigento**. It is the namesake of **Empedocles**, a **Greek pre-Socratic philosopher** and a citizen of the city of **Agrigentum** (present-day **Agrigento**), in his day a Greek colony in **Sicily**. The primary industries of Porto Empedocle are **agriculture**, **fishing**, ironworking, **pharmaceuticals** and rock salt refining.

Born as a port zone in the old Girgenti, today called Agrigento, under the name of Marina di Girgenti (seashore of Girgenti), since in the 15th century it was the main cereal trading centre of the region. From 1549 to 1554, by order of the viceroy Vega, Torre del caricatore of Girgenti, already known during the ancient times (as it probably already existed before the Angevin period), was restored. It had been built to protect against the Saracen pirates, together with the whole system of the Coastal towers of Sicily. The tower was later again restored by Charles III with the help of Bishop Lorenzo Gioeni . This restoration was completed only in 1763. In 1853, during the government of the Kingdom of the Two Sicilies the town obtained independence by becoming chief town of the decurionato under the name of Molo di Girgenti. Then, in 1863, the town changed its name into Porto Empedocle in memory of the Agrigentine philosopher Empedocles.

In 2003, the town changed its official denomination to Porto Empedocle Vigata, after the name of the fictional town where the novels by Andrea Camilleri, Italian writer and native of the town, about detective Inspector Montalbano are placed. However, the decision was revoked in 2009.

The main church is Parrocchia Maria SS.del Buon Consiglio, which is located in the center of the town. The marl Scala dei Turchi is located nearby, on the coast of Realmonte.

Wikipedia

July-29-1943 Thursday – Lacata

The harbor is now getting crowded with cargo ships and L.S.T.'s. We are probably waiting for them to unload. At 16.00 we started to get underway. We have 2 S6. and 2 English gun boats and a couple of L.C.I.

July-30-1943 Friday – Underway

In the morning we pass Pantelleria. At 16.00 we came in site of Cape Bon, (Tunisia Africa). At 23.30 we dropped anchor outside Bizerte.

July-31-1943 Saturday – Lac-De-Bizerte

At 0.600 we pulled into the bay and tied up and discharged the beach parties. The Italian Admiral and General were taken away at 0.800. When they left the ship they turned and threw us an American Salute. At 12.00 chowtime we got underway. We anchor off shore in the bay. We will wait here until we get orders to pull in and have our ship repaired. At 14.00 Harry Johnson, Kenny Horton and others including myself went ashore.

We hitched a ride in an Army truck into the center of Bizerte. We went to a movie which is our first since we left the States. It was a movie house seating about two hundred. We saw "Come Live with Me." with Hedy Lamarr and Jimmy Stewart. After the show we had to hitch another ride to make our ship in time. This was easily done because there are always plenty of trucks running about. When returning to the ship we received our long awaited mail. I received 15 letters.

August-1-1943, Sunday – Lac-De-Bizerte

We had a diver look over our screw today.

August-2-1943, Monday – Lac-De-Bizerte

The diving crew repatched our shaft. We are trying to get by without putting a new shaft in. We then sailed out into the bay and dropped anchor. Things seem to be slack. There are four hospital ships, also lying near us.

August-3-1943 Tuesday – Lac-De-Bizerte

We got paid at 13.00 at which time I drew all my money and sent it home. After being paid Harry Johnson, Ski, and myself went on Liberty in Ferrysville. We left our ship in a big grain boat and boarded an L.C.I. – 194 (Landing Craft Infantry). It was Mr. Frost's ship. We spent sometime talking to him about the other fellows we knew from the Solomons. There was very little to do in Ferryville. We bought grapes which cost $0.80 a bunch. We also had lemonade. We got acquainted with a family who gave us wine. It was a private home. He fought in the last war with France. Although we could not speak the same tongue we managed to understand one another. He showed us pictures of himself in the last war. After we left his home, we went to the busy section and bought more lemonade and fruit. At 20.00 our Liberty expired at 19:00 we headed back to our ship. While aboard the L.C.I. I never saw so many drunks. They were all cut up from fights and falls. The wine we get is very strong and if one take to much it makes you deathly sick. This was the first day I wore my whites. All in all, we had a swell time, even though there wasn't very much to do.

August-4-1943, Wednesday – Lac-De-Bizerte

The diver just finished looking over our shaft again. All I did today was write letters.

August-5-1943, Thursday – Lac-De-Bizerte

It is very dull aboard our ship now. All we do is wait for our Liberty day to come around. The rest of the time we stand our watches and do our work. At night we can see the prison camp. It is well lighted and covers quite a bit of ground.

August-6-1943 Friday – Lac-De-Bizerte

Today was hot as usual. I received mail from dad and Thelm. There are many ships that have been unload and dropped anchor near us. We are waiting for a convoy to go to Oran so we can have are shaft fixed. We are suppose to sail tomorrow.

August-7-1943 Saturday – Lac-De-Bizerte

Last night we had an air raid, which is very unusual. It occurred at 03.45 and ended at 05.30. As usual they dropped flairs lighting up the bay all its surroundings. Several planes dove close to our ships and dropped bombs. They were to far away to do any damage; but the shrapnel landed on our decks. They dropped bombs on the mainland which caused fires that lasted until far in to the late afternoon. It was reported from the beach that we brought done seven planes. One German, four engine bombers flew over our ship at a low altitude. It dropped bombs, then flew on. Because of the darkness, we only saw it for a second, but we heard the bombs whistling for several seconds. This is some sensation being able to hear the plane and hearing bombs whistling, but can't see anything. Our 40 mm jammed at this point which also didn't help the situation any. After eating chow we had Captain's inspection, personal and quarters. At 13.00 we went on Liberty to Bizerte and saw a show. It was "Ziefield Girls", with Lana Turner, Judy Garland and Jimmy Stewart. Because there isn't else to do we returned to our ship after the show. At 20.00 we had mail call, at which received a letter from Ed, Dad, Thelm and others. There was about 25 LS.T.'s loading at the pier, then at night, they made way to the sea. Our plans for getting underway have been changed and now we don't know when we are leaving.

August-8-1943 Sunday – Lac-De-Bizerte
The Higgins are now practicing for another invasion. At mail call I received letters from Mother, Ed, Craine and two from Thelm. At 23.00 we had practice spotting airplanes. It was a practice for the search lights in picking them out.

August-9- Monday – Lac-De-Bizerte
More destroyers are moving into the bay, there was also, a loaded troop ship move in this morning. As it looks, we may make another invasion with our bent screw.

August-10-1943 Tuesday – Lac-De-Bizerte
We are standing four on and eight off. The wind has made the bay rough and because of this we have no swimming from our ship. At 20:00 we heard a broadcast from Tunis. It was a recording of Red Skelton. This is our regular station which brings of news and music.

August -11-1943 Wednesday – Lac-De-Bizerte
I received a letter from the 24th of July. We went on Liberty to Bizerte and show "Reno" with Ric Dex. After the show we came back to Karuba (see map) and saw another show "Twin Beds".

Karuba is a village in **Nord-Kivu, Democratic Republic of the Congo**. In September and October 2007, it was the scene of fighting between the forces of rebel general **Laurent Nkunda** and the **army of the Democratic Republic of the Congo**. The Congolese army claimed to be in control of Karuba as of October 10, 2007

August-12-1943 Thursday – Lac-De-Bizerte

In the morning we went to Ferryville, where we put our ship in dry dock. They fixed the dry dock after being bombed. This will save us a trip to Oran.

After tying up in the dry dock we put the life rafts over and started cleaning the sides of the ship at the water's edge. Although we had more fun than anything.

After chow, we went back to our job, at which time we had a Red Bizerte – A couple of observation planes flew over.

August-13-Friday – Ferryville

At 07:00 they started to leave the water out of the dry dock. It took 6 hours to complete this job. At 13:00 we went over the side to clean off the barnacles. After an hour of this we went swimming in the next dry dock, which is being repaired. Our dry dock has many leaks, but good enough to complete our job. The prisoners are going to paint our ship.

August-14-Saturday – Ferryville

Today they started painting and repairing our ship. They are also fixing the bent shaft. We had a Red Bizerte at 08:00, it was only observation planes.

52

August-15-Sunday – Ferryville

We spent all day in Tunis. Me, Johnson, Ski and myself left at 10:00 by motor car. On the way to Tunis, which is about 70 miles, we passed much German equipment that had been destroyed including planes that had been shot done. I saw several oasis with many camels watering. Tunis is a large city, comparable to some of ours with many modern buildings. While here we saw two shows, "Cat People" and "Eagle Squadron". We stopped at the Red Cross and had our noon "chow". All we had to drink was citrus juice. On the way back our German truck ran our of gas. This made us late. We returned to the ship, I received a letter from Thelm.

August-16- Monday – Lac-De-Bizerte

In the morning they started to empty the dry dock. By 12.00 the lock was opened and we were getting underway. We cruised around the lake to test our screw. After testing we dropped anchor. In the morning at 04.30 we had a Red Bizerte (raid). Planes flew high about, and there was very little activity. At 22.00 enemy planes flew over and dropped bombs which landed near several English ships. This lasted until 22.00 very little action.

August 17, Tuesday – Lac-De-Bizerte

Very little happened thru out the day; but at night things really popped. It all started while I was on watch at 21.30. While everyone was taking their battle stations the enemy dropped flairs. Through the entire raid we were the center of attraction. There was at least ten flairs dropped directly forward of us. The first enemy plane, a bomber was picked up in the search lights and the shore batteries immediately brought it down covered with flames. The bombers came over and dropped trains of bombs of at least ten in a line. As the bombers flew directly over us the search lights played on them and we opened fired. Bombs dropped over our fan tail and along either side paralleled to our ship. It was the closest danger we have yet encountered.

An L.C.I. (Landing Craft Infantry) along with our port quarter tried to escape the bombs. As she was crossing our bow, another string of bombs came down and blew her out of the water. These bombs were intended for us. It was immediately put into flames and the water surrounding it was boiling. The crew was screaming while a near by Liberty ship poured water on her. She was drifting into us we pulled anchor and backed away and while doing this we almost rammed another ship that was sunk during the Bizerte Champaign.

The L.C.I. was at one time right under our bow. It then rolled over and sunk. Out of the whole crew 19 were rescued. While this was going on the bombers were still working on us, and the shrapnel was raining on the decks hitting some, but doing little damage. Fires were lite by the bombs, on the mainland. At 23.00 the raid ended and we were secured. At 05:00, Wednesday that came back but in less volume. This lasted but a half hour causing no damage.

August 18, Wednesday – Lac-De-Bizerte

Today we learned that there were at least, one hundred planes, of which we got seven. The L.C.I #1 was the one that got sunk. A tanker was hit but not sunk. We have almost all the L.S.T.'s in the bay now and we received word to prepare for another invasion. The ships are starting to load now, so we figure it won't be long now. At 22.15 the Gerries, (German's) started their raid for the evening. They dropped more bombs in the bay then they ever did. The bombers were so close to us that our ship was jarred up and down. Once again the shrapnel was flying and I caught one piece on my shin. It was estimated that we brought down ten planes. Beau Fighters (a British long-range heavy fighter, served in WWII, as a night fighter, then as a fighter bomber), intercepted seventeen more. The raid lasted until 24.45. At 03.30 they came back again. They dropped more bombs and flairs. This raid lasted until 04.00.

August 19, Thursday – Lac-De-Bizerte

We noticed great quantities of oil on the water in the morning. Probably a tanker was hit during last night's raids. I went on Liberty again 01.00. First I went to Bizerte to see a show, but the power had been shut off or rather bombed out. We then returned to Karuba and saw Cary Grant and Irene Dunn in "The Awful Truth". We then returned to our ship.

August 20, 1943 Friday – Lac-De-Bizerte

No aid raid last night. The weather these days is terrible hot and we aren't permitted to take our shirts off because of air raids.

August 21, 1943 Saturday – Lac-De-Bizerte

No air raids last night. L.S.T's and L.C.I's have left the lake and have all loaded. They are going on a dry run. We were not among them.

August 22, 1943 Sunday – Lac-De-Bizerte

We had Red Bizerte at 03.00. It lasted but a few minutes. On shore they were shooting up flairs for the entire evening. They are practicing for the next evasion which doesn't seem far off.

August 23, Monday – Lac-De-Bizerte

No air raid last night. We went on Liberty in Karuba and saw a show which was called "Ariel Gunnery" with Richard Arlen. I talked with Hulbgrausm, Lick and others. While on shore we noticed the L.S.T.'s and L.C.I.'s were loading up again.

August 24, 1943 Tuesday – Lac-De-Bizerte

No air raid last night. Today some new L.S.T.'s came into the lake. We are, at present, scraping and painting our ship. The post office has been damaged and therefore has been held up.

August 25, 1943 Wednesday – Lac-De-Bizerte

No air raid last night. Today I received v-mail from Mother. We pulled into the Harbor at 15.00 and put on water. The other L.S.T. crews are moving to new L.S.T.'s. It is rumored they will go to India. We are all hoping we will stay put. There is to much work to be done on a new ship and beside we were supposed to have the best L.S.T. of the group.

August 26, 1943 Thursday – Lac-De-Bizerte

No aid raid last night. We finished loading on water last night. We are also having our #2 davit repaired. At 09.00 we pulled out into the lake and dropped anchor.

August 27, 1943 Friday – Lac-De-Bizerte

We are on Liberty in Karuba. We went to see "Canel Zone" After the show we came back to the ship.

August 28, 1943 Saturday – Lac-De-Bizerte

We are making an all out attempt to paint the ship. At 14.00 had a Red Bizerte at which nothing happened. Our ship is going to be the lead ship of this invasion too. The Ltd. Commander of the Flotilla came aboard with two other Ltd. to direct the invasion.

August 29, 1943 Sunday - Lac-De-Bizerte

We are working as fast as possible to finish the painting on our ship.

August 30, Monday – Lac-De-Bizerte

Last night just before dusk, we docked near the British repair ships, which is next to the oil and ammunition dump. We discharged oil and immediately anchored out in the bay to keep away from the dumps. In the last raid one was blown up and caused quite a fire. We are still having an all-out time of the painting of the ship. We get up at 06:00 and work until 20.00.

August 31, 1943 Tuesday – Lac-De-Bizerte

The raining season is approaching. The sky is clouding up and the wind is beginning to rise. We finished painting topside today and now have to paint the sides.

September 1, 1943 Wednesday – Lac-De-Bizerte

We finished painting starboard side of our ship today. We were given orders were by we must have our ship completed by tomorrow night. Some ships such as, tankers, transports, have pulled out leaving but a few ships beside our invasion force.

September 2, 1943 Thursday – Lac-De-Bizerte

We have almost completed painting our ship.

September 3, 1943 Friday – Lac-De-Bizerte

We finished paint our ship and received word that we are loading tomorrow.

September 4, 1943 Saturday – Lac-De-Bizerte

At 0.600 we got underway and tied up at Karuba. We loaded on British trucks and British soldiers of the famous 8th Army. All day long L.C.T's and L.C.I.'s and all other small landing craft and gun boats steamed out of lake toward the open sea. It seems to be an endless line. At 15.00 we finished loading and now wait orders to move.

September 5, 1943 Sunday – Lac-De-Bizerte

At 17.00 yesterday we moved out to the bay and been there ever since. We with the English aboard have tea between each meal. In the evening our Skipper helped a muster in our quarter and told of our plans. We are striking in 1 hour which is 03.30. It will be Italy. Forty miles north of Naples it our objective in Salerno We will arrive there on the 10th.

September 6, Monday – Lac-De-Bizerte

In the wee hours of the morning twenty-five German paratroopers landed in Bizerte, five of which have already been captured. They started fires in several places. We are getting underway at 10:45, at which time we will anchor out of the bay and wait until tomorrow morning before starting our trip. After the invasion we will ferry between Tripoli *(see map p.60)* and some Italy base. At 20.35 we had an air raid at which time only one bomb came close to us. The raid was in Bizerte. All the ships were anchored out of the bay at this time; thus little damage was done. Some fires were started on the mainland.
The raid was over at 22.00.

September 7, 1943 Tuesday – Anchored Outside of Lac-De-Bizerte

At 06.00 we got underway. We have three flat tops, English and several free French battlewagons and destroyers. The weather is warm with the water fairly choppy. Just before we sailed I received four letters, three from Thelma and one from Mr. Thomas. At 18:00 all is well, we had no trouble at all. All through the day many B-17 passed us coming and going. During the night we passed Sicily.

September 8, 1943 Wednesday – Underway

This morning two convoys came into view and are slowing catching up to make one large convoy. We are heading straight toward Italy. The weather is very good. The water is smooth. We passed several small islands that already belong to us. At 16.00 the L.C.I. convoy joined us.. We broke formation then joined again and are now proceeding toward our destination. There is still another convoy coming up from behind. Just about this time a F.W. 190 came in from behind and dropped several bombs off our fantail. He was very low just off our port side. He then flew halfway up the convoy and then went up out of sight. At about 17:00 we received that three subs were in the vicinity. Shortly after this, one of our leading ships was struck and it sunk before we reached it. At dusk we sighted Isia, an island. We then moved along rather slow. Then we sighted the Isle of Capri *(see map p.62)*. By this time it was dark, with the exception of a half moon. We then moved into the Bay of Salerno. We did not drop anchor. We had land all around us, except where we came in. We were within three miles on our port side, and 18 miles from our Starboard side, where our beach was. We went on General Quarters (GQ) at 18.00, that is when the F.W. (Focke-Wulf 190; a German single seat fighter aircraft) dove on us long before the landings took place. The Germans had us spotted. The usual tactics followed. Flairs were first dropped then the bombs. Immediately we knocked one of their planes over and then more followed. The

Roberts, and English Battlewagon, was just ahead of us and it put up a good barrage. It was hot and heavy all night long. At day break the first planes we sighted was out P38's planes a very much welcome sight. Everyone let out a sigh of relief. Only once in a while a German plane would slip in and then would cause little damage.

September 9, 1943 Thursday – Bay of Salerno

We are still at general quarters. We are supposed to beach at 11:00. Every time we tried to beach, the German's 88's opened up and chased us out again.   We did this all day. When the effrontery landed, after the commandoes, the German's brought out tanks, which they had buried and cause quite a bit of trouble. The battlewagon's opened fire and drove the German's in land.

September 10, 1943 Friday – Bay of Salerno (see map p.64)

Last night at 24.00 we were secured from G.Q. (General Quarters). We managed to get four hours sleep in. Then we had another air attack. We beached our ship at 07.15. We did a good job; it went up high and dry. At 8:15 we were out in the bay again. We missed our convoy, at 7.45 and now have to wait until another convoy is formed. While waiting to unload on the 9, a sea going tug brought over a hundred wounded men aboard. They were all burned and some shell shocked. Two of these died while on board. We discharged forty by small boats and after completing beach operations, we tied up a long side of the 400 and discharged the rest. Although we have four on and four off we are almost constantly at our guns. It is now 7.30 (19.30) and time to go on watch. This is the first chance I had to sit still and even now I was just interrupted by a G.Q. Everyone is almost exhausted. While on watch we had G.Q. 20.30. At 23.30 during G.Q., we got underway. We made our way away from the firing and out to sea. We are traveling SW with our destination unknown. During the invasion, we lost quite a few ships, three L.S.T. were destroyed by fire while unloading on the beach and others were shot up pretty bad. We were very fortunate again and escaped without injury thus far.

September 11, 1943 Saturday

Underway nothing happened through the night. At 18.00 we passed the Island of Ustica (see map p.65). We are not going through the straight as planned, probably because they is to much action. Our destination is still unknown. The convoy are traveling with will not tell us were we are heading. At 22.00 we were told we are heading toward, Lac De Bizerte.

September 12, 1943 Sunday – Lac De Bizerte

Scores and scores of bombers passed us all day long heading to and from Italy. At 17.00 we dropped anchored outside Lac De Bizerte. Our trips to ad from Italy was made of glass like water. We are still on Condition II.

September 13, 1943 Monday – Lac De Bizerte

Early in the morning at 07.00 we moved into the channel. On the way we received word to dock and be loaded by 24 hrs. The LCT's and the LCI's left late last night. We are now waiting for our load. It is now 15.00 and all we did so far was put on water and fuel. Our cook has received word to cook for 500. By 18.00 our trucks were rolling on. At 23.00 we lifted anchor and sailed out of the bay to join the convoy. We have 70 American boys are the rest English, about 250.

September 14, 1943 Tuesday – Underway

We are all underway with smooth sailing. At 12:00 we were passing Ustica (a tiny volcano island off Sicily's north coast.) By 17.00 we were passing Salerno, Italy.

Tripoli

Tripoli is the capital city and the largest city of Libya, with a population of about 1.158 million people in 2018. It is located in the northwest of Libya on the edge of the desert, on a point of rocky land projecting into the Mediterranean Sea and forming a bay. It includes the port of Tripoli and the country's largest commercial and manufacturing centre. It is also the site of the University of Tripoli. The vast Bab al-Aziziabarracks, which includes the former family estate of Muammar Gaddafi, is also located in the city. Colonel Gaddafi largely ruled the country from his residence in this barracks.

Tripoli was founded in the 7th century BC by the Phoenicians, who named it *Oea*. Due to the city's long history, there are many sites of archaeological significance in Tripoli. *Tripoli* may also refer to the *shabiyah* (top-level administrative division in the current Libyan system), the Tripoli District.

Tripoli is also known as **Tripoli-of-the-West** to distinguish it from its Phoenician sister city Tripoli, Lebanon, known in Arabic as *Ṭarābulus al-Sham*, meaning "Levantine Tripoli". It is affectionately called "The Mermaid of the Mediterranean", describing its turquoise waters and its whitewashed buildings. Tripoli is a Greek name that means "Three Cities"

Wikipedia

September 15, 1943 Wednesday – Underway

Last night we received word that our forces were diving well and that the Germans' have increased their air power. We are going to land at Salerno again. It is now 08.00 and we are going to land at 13.00. We have been running at 10 knots, the fastest we ever did. Their convoy is carrying N/4 tanker and can be busters. We held GQ (general quarters) at 09.45. We arrived here earlier than expected. The city lies just ahead beyond a fog bank. While approaching the city our port engine gave out. While filling us with oil, they gave us salt water too. We then got it running again. We then started to enter the harbor as expected; but the 88's, s started once again and drove us out. They were flying on all sides and across our ship. All we could hear was a whistle, then a bang and then a spout of water shot high into the air. We tried and tried to enter but was driven out to see each time. While this was going on our naval and also British war ships were also firing into shore. We then went up the beach, close to where we were before and made a landing, another good one. At this point there was many tanks destroyed, that is enemy. While we were making the first invasion they came to the beach and fired at us and other destroyers fired and knock them out. Our unloading to longer their due to the many small trailers. We landed at 1.45 and completed our job by 15.30 and then pulled off the beach and moved off shore and dropped anchor. Even at this time, 16.00 is quiet with little action from our battlewagon once in a while.

It is now 19.00 and we are still anchored several miles off shore. We just finished another air raid at which we got two enemy planes. Hundreds and Hundreds of our planes keep coming and going. At 21.30 we had G.Q. (General Quarters), which lasted all night. While on GQ we could hear long continuous rumbles caused by our bombs dropping from our planes. We can also see lightening going on back and forth on the beach.

September 16, 1943 Thursday – Underway

This morning more enemy raids came over of which we got one.   At 08.00 we were secured from G.Q. (General Quarters), but were kept running back and forth all morning by the alerts. At 11.00 we formed our convoy consisting all of L.S.T's. We are heading for Tripoli.

Gulf of Naples

The **Gulf of Naples**, also called the **Bay of Naples**, is a roughly 15-kilometer-wide (9.3 mi) gulf located along the south-western coast of Italy (province of Naples, Campaniaregion). It opens to the west into the Mediterranean Sea. It is bordered on the north by the cities of Naples and Pozzuoli, on the east by Mount Vesuvius, and on the south by the Sorrento Peninsula and the main town of the peninsula, Sorrento. The Peninsula separates the Gulf of Naples from the Gulf of Salerno, which includes the Amalfi Coast.

The islands of Capri, Ischia and Procida are located in the Gulf of Naples. The area is a tourist destination, with the seaside Roman ruins of Pompeii and Herculaneum at the foot of Mount Vesuvius (destroyed in the AD 79 eruption of Vesuvius), along the north coast.

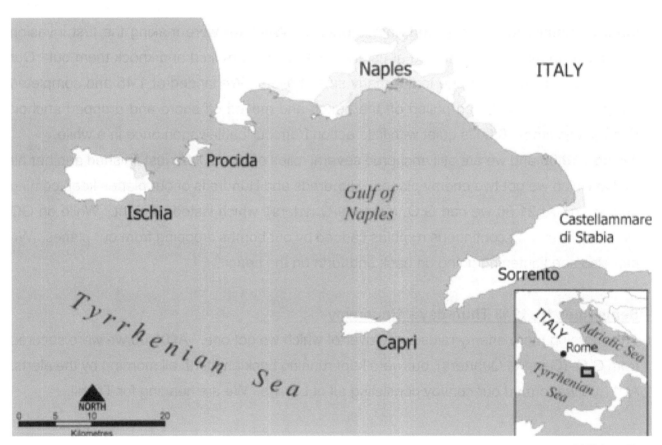

Wikipedia

September 17, 1943 Friday – Underway

Everything is running along smoothly including the weather. By 02.00 we were passing through the Straits of Messina. There was a nine knot current with us.

September 18, 1943 Saturday – Underway

Today our steering broke and the ship had to be steered thru the Executive Steering Room. In the last two days we sighted no airplanes. It is now 17.00 and we are forming our convoy into two lanes to go through the mine fields to Tripoli. At dusk we dropped anchor outside of Tripoli. It lies on the edge of the desert. There are no hills. It is flat land with palm trees.

September 19, 1943 Sunday – Tripoli

In the morning we lifted anchor and sailed into the harbor and tied up next to our hospital ship. As soon as we finished tying up half of the crew was granted Liberty of which Johnson and I were part of. This was our best Liberty yet. After buying souvenirs' and such we met two soldiers in a jeep. They showed us old Tripoli as well as new Tripoli. New Tripoli has very wide streets and modern buildings. There are no high buildings. We were talked out of convoy duty, with unknown orders.

September 20, 1943 Monday – Tripoli

We tied up at the dock today and began loading English soldiers and American equipment. At 17.00 we finished loading and at 18.00 we left the docks to anchor outside the breakwater. By 19.30 we were underway there are ten L.S.T.'S and again we don't know where we are heading.

September 21, 1943 Tuesday – Underway

The weather is very warm and the water calm. We're heading toward the Straits of Messina due North. It is now late afternoon and as usual nothing has happened. Making this trip now is just an everyday acquaintance.

September 22, 1943 Wednesday – Underway

At 15.00 we started entering the Straits. It is very easy to see both sides. While entering we saw Mt. Edna. It will take us several hours to pass through these straits. There are small cities scattered along the shores and among the hills through the entire strait. At 17.00 we left the straits.

September 23, 1943 Thursday – Salerno

In the morning at 05.15 we had G.Q (General Quarters). We held this until daybreak. At 09.00 we were in the bay outside Salerno. There was no action at all. We were secured from G.Q. (General Quarters). At 12.00 we tried to beach our ship but hit a sandbar and had to try again, at which time we made it. We unloaded in about thirty minutes and then moved into the bay and waited for the rest. By 17.00 we were underway and heading back to Tripoli with the same ships as we came with.

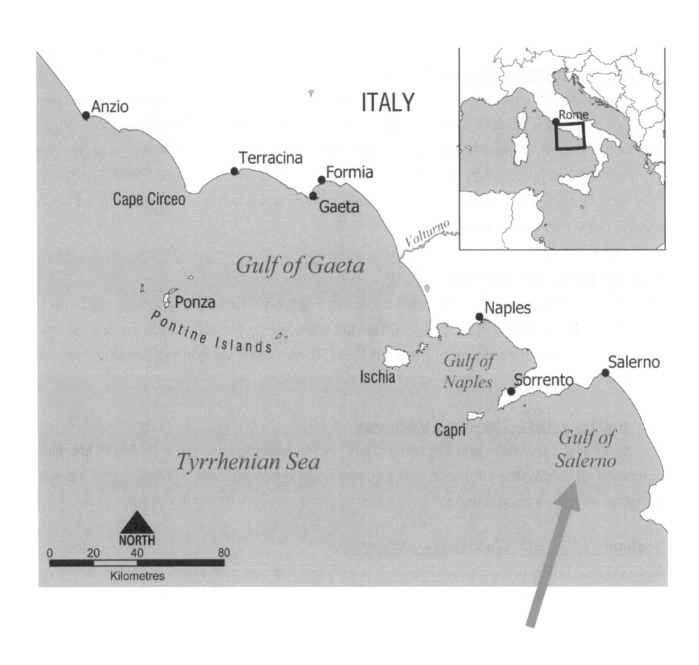

September 24, 1943 Friday — Underway

We are following the shore line as like the last time. While passing the volcano Stromboli (on a small island, north of Sicily) (*see map*); we saw it erupting. High flames and pillars of smoke high in the air. From 11.00 – 13.00 we were passing through the Straits of Messina.

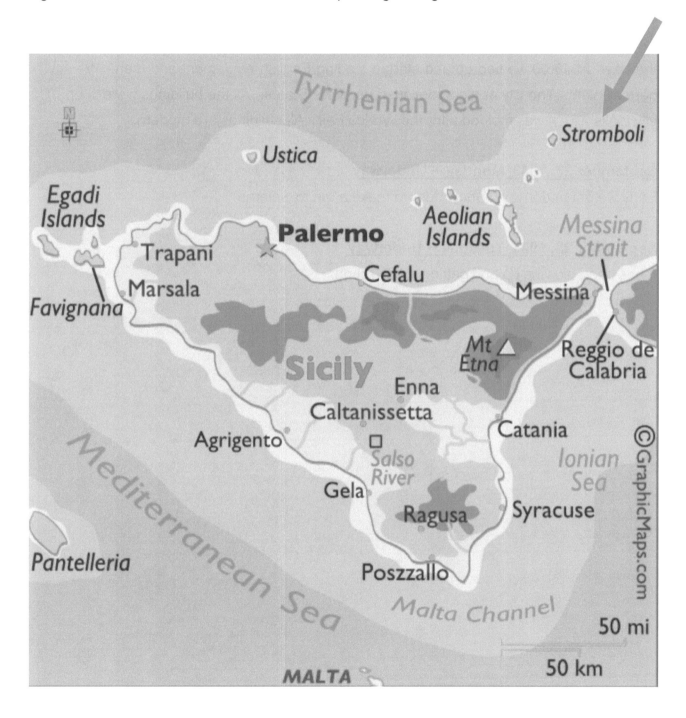

September 25, 1943 Saturday — Underway

The weather is swell. It is very warm and the water is almost like glass.

September 26, 1943 Sunday — Underway

This morning we sited land and Tripoli. We pulled in next to an oil tender and put on oil. It took about half hour, after which we tied up next to another L.S.T. anchored in the center of the bay. At 18.00 we tied up and started loading English equipment and men. We stayed here all night. The city at night reminded us of the States. All the buildings were lit up. The city looks as if it was molded after the Worlds Fair. All buildings are modern.

September 27. 1943 Monday — Underway

Early we got underway. Once more to make a trip to Salerno.

September 28, 1943 Tuesday — Underway

It has been blowing up and getting pretty rough.

Salerno landing in Italy

September 29, 1943   Wednesday – Underway

At midnight we went through the straits. At 17.00 with rough weather still prevailing we sited land; – the Bay of Salerno. We pulled in close and dropped anchor.

Sept 30, 1943 Thursday Bay of Salerno

Last night was very cold. We waited all day to pull in, our chance came at 18.00. This landing was successful. We landed at some what the same place. During this completed operation we had no action. At dusk, 19.30 we pulled out of the beach and made our way to the out skirts of the anchored ships and then dropped anchor.

October 1, 1943 Friday – Bay of Salerno

We laid over in the bay all night. By 0.900 we got underway with nine L.S.T.'s and started on our way. We believe we are going to Tripoli again although we are supposed to go to Bizerte. All L.S.T.'s must be in Lac-De-Bizerte by the 15 of the month, probably for another invasion. There has been a rumor that sixty L.S.T.'s will go to India; some are on their way. We will probably be the next group to go.

Oct. 2, 1943 Saturday – Underway

From our ship we could see Stromboli, erupting again. It was very dark and with the sundown burst of flames shooting skyward made a beautiful picture. From 0.300 to 0.500 we were passing through the straits. We have left sight of all land. The rainy season is coming. It gets very cold at night with some sprinkles forming. At evening chow we had a real electric storm. We missed most of it. By 19.00 we had out ridden it.

October 3, 1943 Sunday – Underway

We had fairly nice weather today. We will pull into Tripoli sometime tonight. We pulled in after dark. We were guided by two search lights. The town was light up the same as before. We dropped anchor out beyond breakwater.

October 4, 1943 Monday –Tripoli

At 10.00 we pulled inside and tied up next to an oiler and put on fuel. When completed we dropped anchor in the harbor to wait for loading orders. We were reminded that we must be in Lac- De-Bizerte by the 15th. At dusk we loaded. We are carrying American volunteers of an ambulance division of England and we are carrying no infantry.

October 5, 1943 Tuesday – Underway

At sunup we were underway. We are not going to Salerno. We will go to Taranto (Gulf of Tranto, *see map p.67*) in the end of the "boot". Our days are getting cloudy with occasional rain.

October 6, 1943 Wednesday – Underway

This morning at dawn we had G.Q. (General Quarters) Nothing happened.

October 7, 1943 Thursday – Underway

We now have G.Q. (General Quarters) at sunup and sundown. We are heading toward the "heel" of Italy in the Gibraltar Sea (*see map*). We will be fifty miles from Greece. All we have is a P.C.& S.C. (Patrol Coastal & Submarine Chaser, see picture on page 39), for protection.

October 8, 1943 Friday – Taranto

We could see landfall all morning. At 09.30 we started entering the Bay to Taranto. Taranto was one of the biggest Naval Base that they had. While entering the base we passed thru many subnets. To enter this base we had to pass thru a manmade canal. It was guarded at the entrance by two old fashion forts on either side of the entrance. This sides of the entrance were about 60' high, with a drawbridge connecting them. While passing through many Italians were lined up on both sides to see the Americans and our big landing craft. We are the first Americans to enter here. We then pulled into the lake, where we dropped anchor to await orders to unload here. There were many Italian war ships in here, including heavy cruisers and light ones about twenty subs and more being built in the shipyards and countless numbers of destroyers. Attached to their lake is another lake, which is used as a Naval Aircraft Base. There is also, a group of large landing fields nearby. Our C47's are constantly landing and departing. They are bringing back wounded from the front lines.

At 16.30 we moved across the lake and tied up next to a shipyard where several ships are under construction, as we were. It is dark now and unloading is now taking place.

Strait of Gibraltar

October 9, 1943 Saturday – Taranto

We moved out into the middle of the lake last night. And this morning at daybreak we passed through the channel and into the outer harbor and continued on our way back to Lac – De-Bizerte, home.

October 10, 1943 Sunday – Underway

We are having excellent sailing weather. In the afternoon we passed by Malta.

October 11, 1943 Monday – Underway

This afternoon we passed by Pantelleria, (*see map*) and also came within sight of Africa. We have just passed Lake Bon and now are preparing to enter Bizerte. Harry Johnson received word today that he will be transferred to Kurba (a Croation Island in the Adriatic Sea used for supply efforts) and possible to the States.

At dusk we anchored outside of Bizerte. We immediately sent our small boat for our long-awaited mail. It has been one month since we have received any mail. We stayed up most of the night reading it.

October 12, 1943 Tuesday – Lac-De-Bizerte

We pulled into the inner harbor today and dropped anchor near the docks. Harry was supposed to leave us, but didn't as yet. There are many changes taken place aboard our ship. Kenny and Dave are supposed to go back to the States. We took our pay accounts and health records aboard. It is rumored that we will make several trips to Italy then go to England. They are transferring extra men. This means that we will not make another invasion for a while at least.

October 13, 1943 Wednesday – Lac-De-Bizerte

We are waiting for the paymaster, after which time Harry will leave us. We waited all day and nothing happened.

Pantelleria

October 14, 1943 Thursday – Lac-De-Bizerte

At 11.00 I went a shore with Harry. We left him at the dispensary. While there we notice the "Liames (English)" loading up with the American soldiers and equipment. There are many ships here. It looks a lot of another evasion, probably Greece.

October 15 Friday – Lac-De-Bizerte

Today I went over to see Harry. Some L.S.T.'s are now heading for England; we are also to go, we are told; but not until we have completed a couple of trips to Italy. Our new skipper came aboard. In the evening a couple fellows, Chris, Layton, Larson, and myself went to a smoker. There was a musical entertainment and also boxing bouts to complete the evening.

October 16, 1943 Saturday – Lac-De-Bizerte

We are now anchored outside the breakwater, all loaded and waiting for sailing orders. We are now underway and passing by Pantelleria.

October 17, 1943 Sunday – Underway

We are now in sight of Sicily with good weather with the exception of a few hard rain storms.

October 18, 1943 Monday – Underway

We are traveling up the coast of Italy and now we are entering the bay outside Taranto. We dropped anchor just off shore. While waiting for orders, to unload I went on Liberty with Ken, Ski, and Hart. We had a good time looking over the place. There was plenty of wine. At dusk we ventured over to old Taranto which is just across the canal. It is very gloomy over there. The streets are like alleys about 5' wide. It is dirty and has many strong odors. While here it began to rain. It became very dark and the rain turned into a downpour. We had at least two miles to walk to our ship. This was the first Liberty with our dress blues. We returned to the ship on time.

October 19, 1943 Tuesday – Taranto

We did not enter the bay to unload instead we unloaded at a pier in old Taranto. While unloading many of the fellows bought watches. On the main road directly in front of us was and less line of Italians migrating back to the city from the hills.

In the afternoon, we anchored off shore again. At 17.00 we got underway with mild weather.

October 20, 1943 Wednesday – Underway

It is calm and warm, we as yet do not know where we are going.

October 21, 1943, Thursday – Underway

We passed Pantelleria (an island in the Strait of Sicily; SW of Sicily and E. of Tunisian; (*see map p.73*) during the day.

October 22. 1943 Friday – Underway

Before dawn we passed Cap Bon (see map p.76) and by daybreak we are entering Bizerte. We came right in and dropped anchor in the bay. In the afternoon we attempted to tie up. After four hours of trying to fight against the high wind, we gave up and secured the ship as it was to finish the job when the wind had died down.

October 23, 1943 – Bizerte, Kurba (a Croatian Island)

In the morning we sighted the ship to start loading. All afternoon I stayed over the hospital with Harry. When I returned we had orders to get underway, but because the Liberty party was still out we couldn't leave. They sent a truck after them but didn't get them all, we then got delayed sailing orders. Because I promised Johnson I would be back the next day, I went to see him, after dark. After I left him I went to see the show "Joe Smith America".

October 24, 1943 – Lac-De-Bizerte

At 06.00 we got underway with another L.S.T. and two S.C. (Signal Corps, is an Army Signal man who is well versed in radio and visual communications) We are going to Oran. We believe we are taking supplies to Naples.

October 25, 1943 – Underway

We are running into some bad weather and we also had some reports of sub and aircraft activity in the vicinity.

October 26, 1943 – Underway

Today we passed by Bougie.

Cape Bon

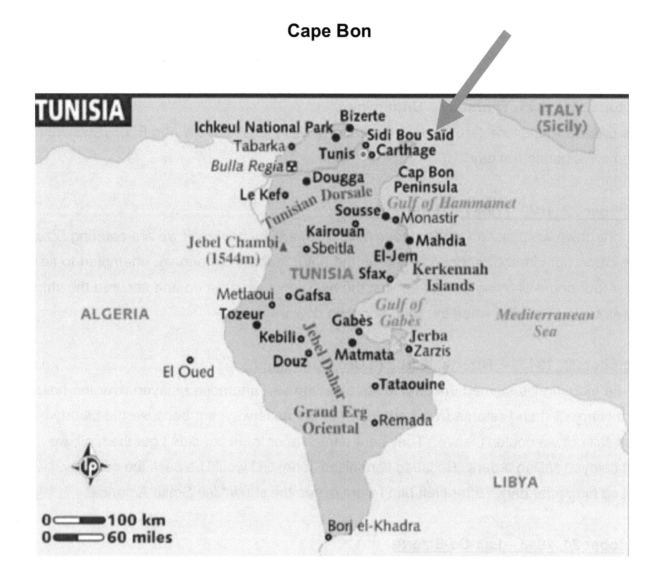

Cape Bon is the peninsula in far northeastern Tunisia, near Sicily. The naval **Battle of Cape Bon** took place on December 13, 1941 during the **Second World War**, between two **Italian** light cruisers and an Allied **destroyer** flotilla off **Cape Bon, Tunisia**.

October 27, 1943 - Oran

We arrived in Oran. It is the largest Army Depot in North Africa. The French battleway Richlear is also here. We made Liberty from 13.00 to 22.00. On Liberty with Ski, we had our first glass of beer since landing in N.A. (North Africa). It isn't' a bad Liberty town. The prices are very high on everything. We saw the picture "Take A Little Darling" with Shirley Temple.

October 28, 1943 – Oran

All night long they dropped depth charges. In the afternoon we tied up an started loading M4's (M4 Sherman, medium tank, was the primary battle tank used by the United States) and haft tracks. (A half-track is a military vehicle with regular wheels at the front for steering and continuous track s at the back to propel).

October 29, 1943 – Oran

All the other L.S.T.'s except the ones that are going to England, are loading up with M'4s. and half-tracks. There is quite a bit of talk of an "evasion" behind the lines, probably North of Rome. We are all loaded. We are stilled tied up at the pier. We had to pull out at 17.00.

At 18.30 we started to pull out when another L.S.T., also getting underway, collided into our aft gun turret putting it out of commission and ripping a hole in our side; however, the damage is mild and will not cause us to layover in Oran. We are first going to Bizerte.

October 30, 1943 – Underway

We have five escorts for the four L.S.T.'s. We are carrying our best tank division, 1st Army, 4th division.

October 31. 1943 Sunday – Underway

We are still following the coast and are having fine weather.

November 1, 1943 – Lac-De-Bizerte

Upon arriving at Bizerte, we ran into sub trouble. Mine sweeps dropped the depth charges with in 300 feet of our ship. This took place just outside Bizerte Harbor. We pulled into the Harbor and refueled and then took off again. Many L.C.T. (Landing Craft Tank) and L.S.T.'s are a head of us. We are trying to catch them. It is now 18.00 and very dark and are still far behind. By 22.00 we caught up to the convoy. The L.S.T. that rammed us, remained at Bizerte. She probably strung her doors.

November 2, 1943 Tuesday – Underway

We passed by Sicily in the afternoon. We practiced maneuvers today during which time an L.C.I. (Landing Craft Infantry) rammed another causing damage to both ships but it did not stop them from keeping underway.

November 3, 1943 Wednesday – Naples

We arrived at Naples in the morning and immediately, started to discharge our tanks. After we finished our unloading we waited for the rest, after which time we were allowed to wander in the vicinity. In the afternoon we had an air alert with distant ack-ack fire in the distance. Before dark we got underway and headed out to sea.

November 4, 1943 Thursday – Underway

We are traveling fastest ever. Our nights are cold which during the day it is still nice and warm.

November 5, 1943 Friday – Bizerte, Karuba, (a Croatian Island)

We anchored in the bay outside the breakwater and sent in a small boat for mail. I received three Christmas packages and bulletins. (Croatia is a country at the crossroads of Central and Southeast Europe, on the Adriatic Sea. It has an area of 21,851 square miles and a population of only 4.28 million.)

November 6, 1943 Saturday – Bizerte, Karuba

We are waiting to get our gyro fixed, which was broke when our ship was rammed. We heard that we will be here for a week. Our mail has been sent to Oran. Harry Johnson came aboard today.

November 7, 1943 Sunday – Bizerte, Karuba

This morning Al Legler came over to see me. He ate chow with us and late in the evening he came back to say goodbye for he is loading on and L.S.T. and embarking to England. We are having plenty of rain.

November 8, 1943 Monday – Bizerte

Roesitte came aboard to see us. We are still have driving rains. Near noon time Larry Sandeaver came aboard. We spent the morning looking over my ship. He ate chow with us and in the evening, we went to see a movie. After returning to the ship we had the pleasure of having Floyd Chastain and his banjo, accordion and a guitar played some music. Floyd is from "WHO's YOUR HOT SHOOTS" from the radio. They played all evening, then had to return to their quarters.

November 9, 1943 Tuesday – Bizerte Karuba

We are still waiting to get our gun turret fixed. At evening they started working on the turret.

November 10, 1943 Wednesday – Bizerte Karuba

Our turret won't be fixed for we are leaving tomorrow of Oran.

November 11, 1943 Thursday – Bizerte Karuba

We anchored out in the outer harbor in the morning. By the afternoon, we were underway toward Oran. There is eleven L.S.T.'s with a destroyer escort. The air is chilly and the water rough.

November 12, 1943 Friday – Underway

We ran into rough weather. The sides of our ship were dripping water.

November 13, 1943 Saturday – Underway

The weather has made a change for the better. We have four on and eight off which gives us a little more time for ourselves.

November 13, 1943 Saturday - Underway

Sailing rather smooth.

ORAN, ALGERIA

November 14, 1943 Sunday – Oran

By 16.00 we were in Oran. We anchored out until day and then proceeded into the harbor where we tied up and immediately began to load. We are loading with Frenchmen.

November 15, 1943 Monday – Oran

Our biggest problem is if we will get mail or not. After mail was brought aboard and sorted I received a package from church and one from Thelm, a lot of bulletins. We are tied up next to barges that are full of supplies. It was very convenient for us. We got scores of boxes of candy, field jackets, knives, sweaters etc.

November 16, 1943, Tuesday – Oran

We are still tied up and supplies are still coming aboard. We are having windy weather. We are being held up here to the rough weather.

November 17, 1943 Wednesday – Oran

In the morning we got underway we caught the ships anchored next to us causing us to drift into some more supply barges. We then got a few more supplies. When free we move to the other harbor and dropped anchor. At 19.00 we got underway in Bizerte. The weather is chilly and the water fairly rough.

November 18, 1943 Thursday – Underway

Our passengers, French, Spanish, are very dirty. We have our ship locked off so as to keep them from associated with us. Today we ran into hail and heavy rain.

November 19, 1943 Friday – Underway

We are having smooth sailing. At 17.00 a large convoy of Liberty and tanker ships were passing us during which time they had as well as we sub attack. A smoke screen was put done which was very effective. They are now dropping depth charges in the entire areas. As yet no ships were hit. One sub was seen and that was a French. Activity went on until after dark then all was quite.

November 20, 1943 Saturday – Underway

Today another French sub surfaced and is now tagging alone behind us. We are just outside of Bizerte.   We are due at 0.900. It is now 10.00 and we are anchored outside Bizerte. We laid around all the rest of the day. We went for mail, but received about 10 letters for the whole crew. We are once again underway with good sailing weather. Our destination is unknown.

November 21, 1943 Sunday – Underway

We are now off the coast of Italy proceeding to Naples.

November 22, 1943 Monday – Naples

Coming up toward Naples we saw Mt. Vesuvius. At the bottom of the active volcano lies the city of Naples.   The smoke from Mt. Vesuvius (*see map p.83*) curls high and far.   We proceeded to unload at the Northern end of Naples. We had two air alerts while unloading. After which we proceeded to move up in the bay and drop anchor where we will lay all night. It is very dark and traveling is difficult. All through the day it is very warm.

November 23, 1943 Tuesday – Naples

We are still anchored in the bay. During the night a storm came up causing us to almost drift on the rocks. We are staying here due to the storm. We dropped anchor and the chain broke. In the afternoon we got underway against a rough sea.

November 24, 1943 Wednesday – Underway

We are having great difficulties weathering the sea. Our ship is just about holding together.

November 25, 1943 Thursday – Thanksgiving Day – Underway

The sea calmed down some, so as to let us enjoy our Thanksgiving meal. We were supposed to be in Bizerte this morning but due to the bad weather we could make only 3 knots. We had an excellent meal.

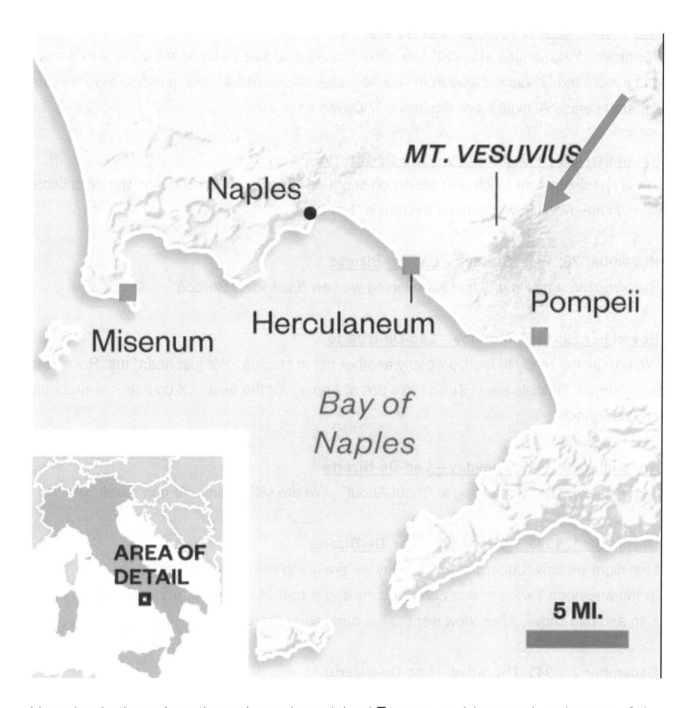

Vesuvius is the only active volcano in mainland **Europe**, and has produced some of the continent's largest volcanic eruptions. Located on Italy's west coast, it overlooks the Bay and City of Naples and sits in the crater of the ancient Somma volcano. Vesuvius is most famous for the 79 AD eruption which destroyed the Roman cities of Pompeii and Herculaneum. Though the volcano's last eruption was in 1944, it still represents a great danger to the cities that surround it, especially the busy metropolis of Naples.

November 26, 1943 Friday – Lac-De-Bizerte

We arrived this morning at 0.400. We moved to the docks at 14.00 near the Delta to get our gun turret fixed. I was secured from watches, special sea details and musters to work in the compartments. At night I saw the movie "7 Days Leave".

November 27, 1943 Saturday – Lac-De-Bizerte

We aren't doing very much, just taking on supplies. The weather is cloudy with occasional rain. In the evening we attended the movie "Hot Spot"

November 28, 1943, Sunday – Lac-De-Bizerte

Received more mail today and the evening we saw "Lucky Mr. Gordon".

November 29. 1943 Monday – Lac-De-Bizerte

We are getting ready to load, probably another trip to Naples. We just heard that Roosevelt and German Officials are in Tunis. We are all hoping for the best. Of course, it is probably another rumor.

November 30, 1943 Tuesday – Lac-De-Bizerte

Last night we saw "Something to Shout About". We are still getting our gun turret fixed.

December 1, 1943 Wednesday – Lac-De-Bizerte

Last night we saw "Underground". Today we are going to load more English.
In the afternoon I went to see Larry and making a tour of his camp, and came back to my ship and had chow. After chow went to the army shoe "Yard Bird".

December 2, 1943 Thursday – Lac-De-Bizerte

As yet there is no notice as to loading. In the evening we attended the show "Du Barry was a Lady". When we came back, we had already begun to load. We are carrying aviation ground crews.

December 3, 1943 Friday – Lac-De-Bizerte

We saw the show "Five Came Back"

December 4, 1943 Saturday – Lac-De-Bizerte

Today we got underway. I spoke with Al McIntyre. We are having wonderful weather.

84

December 5, 1943 Sunday – Underway

We have been off the coast of Sicily all day and making good time with fair weather with the exception of last night when it became very rough causing us to almost loose one of our small boats.

December 6, 1943 Monday – Naples

In the morning before sunup, we could see buildings glowing on the horizon and then a little later we came very close to the isle of Capri also insight of Vesuvius which was also smoking. By this time, it was getting light and we were entering Naples. After docking, Kenny and myself took up and visited a small village. We went into buildings which previous held German and Italian troops. Their clothes were lying all about us. We then visited some wine cellars built into the side of the mountain.

We came back in time to eat chow and then we were off again, this time to the City. This city so far was the best. We bought plenty of nuts and oranges. We met a soldier who showed us the town. While Kenny and I were in town we picked up a mandolin in good condition. When we came back our ship was unloaded and we had taken on 50 Germans to be taken back to Africa to be tried for murder. They buried 40 some Italians a live.

It is now 19.00 and we just had an air alert after which we pulled away from the docks to anchor out until tomorrow.

December 7, 1943 Tuesday – Naples

We had no air alerts last night. It is now 11.00, we are getting underway. The weather is still wonderful. We had the German prisoners helping us do our work. They do their job well. We took the mandolin and guitar up to them and they played us some German songs.

December 8, 1943 Wednesday – Underway

Water very calm and air very warm.

December 9, 1943 Thursday – Underway

The prisoners are learning our ship top to bottom. In the evening they gave us some entertainment on the tank deck. They sang songs of when they were in Africa with Rommel and when they were marching through, Belgian, France and other countries.

December 10, 1943 Friday – Lac-De-Bizerte

We made good time and arrived at Bizerte in the morning. We immediately tied up and discharged our prisoners. In the evening we saw the show "Shanghais Question".

December 11, 1943 Saturday – Lac-De-Bizerte

We moved out in the lake.

December 12, 1943 Sunday – Lac-De-Bizerte

Today I started painting the washing quarters.

December 13, 1943 Monday – Lac-De-Bizerte

Today we pulled next to the Delta at which time I met Jonny Hayes. Most of the day going through his ship and in the evening we saw the picture "New New York City".

December 14, 1943 Tuesday – Lac-De-Bizerte

The Delta put 150 sacks in our tank deck and also did minor repairs. This day too, I spent with Hayes and in the evening we saw "Stage for Canteen".

December 15, 1943 Wednesday – Lac-De-Bizerte

We pulled away from the Delta and anchored in the bay. We are changing our design on the ship probably for another invasion.

December 16, 1943 Thursday – Lac-De-Bizerte

We have our engine ripped down for general overhaul . After assembling they ran into trouble which will take at least four days to fix.

December 17, 1943 Friday – Lac-De-Bizerte

We are giving our ship a complete overhaul, painting, fixing, etc.

December 18, 1943 Saturday – Lac-De-Bizerte

Still working.

December 19, 1943 Sunday – Lac-De-Bizerte

I went to Delta to dentist, then the rest of the day with John. We received three more packages from Mom, Ed, and Mrs. Smith.

December 20, 1943 Monday – Lac-De-Bizerte

Our small boats went on maneuvers. Another invasion seems in season.

December 21, 1943 Tuesday – Lac-De-Bizerte

I received two more packages from Mrs. Kendig and also Aunt Anna. In the evening we saw a double feature. Western and one of Brooklyn.

December 22, 1943 Wednesday – Lac-De-Bizerte

Today they brought pontoons along side to practice with them. It was too late; therefore, it was postponed until tomorrow. We tied up at the dock to take on water. In the evening we saw "Edge of Darkness" with Anne Sheridan and Errol Flynn.

December 23, 1943 Thursday – Lac-De-Bizerte

We moved out of the lake this morning to practice landings with the pontoons. We missed the convoy this trip because of our engines. Met Buckly, saw *Joe and Ethel Turp Call on the President*

(This is a 1939 American comedy film directed by Robert B. Sinclair and written by Melville Baker. The film stars Ann Sothern, Lewis Stone, Walter Brennan, William Gargan, Marsha Hunt and Tom Neal. The film was released on December 1, 1939, by Metro-Goldwyn-Mayer.)

Wikipedia

December 24, 1943 Friday – Lac-De-Bizerte

We turned in all our fire arms. Tonight we are attending a party held for our ship.

December 25, 1943 Saturday – Lac-De-Bizerte

We all had a good time at our party. We had wine, and some French Girls. We had an excellent meal for Christmas. We had turkey, ice cream, and pie and etc.

December 26, 1943 Sunday – Lac-De-Bizerte

We are loading up today with more English Troops. I received more mail from October and November. In the evening we saw "Apache Trail".

December 27, 1943 Monday – Underway

Left Bizerte in the morning with 32 L.C.I and eight L.S.T.'s. Weather fair.

December 28, 1943 Tuesday – Lac-De-Bizerte

Weather still fair. Listen to Bob Hope from a broadcast from Palermo.

December 29, 1943 Wednesday - Naples

We arrived at dusk and unloaded. Kay and I went ashore.

December 30, 1943 Thursday – Naples

At 10.00 we got underway. It was a beautiful day. White smoke was curling down the sides of Vesuvius.

December 31, 1943 Friday – Underway

We ran into the roughest weather. The other L.S.T.'s were braking up and going out of control. At 18.00 the S.C.'s could stay with us and by 24.00, P.C. had to leave and by 04.00 we had to turn around head for Palermo. We couldn't make any progress against the high waves.

January 1, 1944 Saturday – Palermo

We made this by 16.00. We dropped anchor to wait until the storm passes over.

January 2, 1944 Sunday –   Palermo

Although it is bright and warm, the water is still very rough so rough that we can not go beyond the breakwater. We are compelled to lie at anchor and weather the storm. This city is much like the others except for the snow-covered mountains, which I suppose has been covered to the sudden storm we just encountered.

January 3, 1944 Monday – Underway

We were underway early with good sailing weather.

January 4, 1944 Tuesday – Underway

We met more rough weather; which made us arrive late in the afternoon. We made an attempt to enter the harbor, but had to withdrawal because of darkness. After dark we received word to proceed to Tunis to get away from the coming storm. Our anchor caught a cable which made us layover until the next day.

January 5, 1944 Wednesday – Bizerte

We tried to get our anchor up again, but no go. We will have to ride out the storm. At present we have a very high wind. Later our chain broke. The base sent us to Tunis with no mail. We made Tunis in six hours; we had a very high tail wind. We met the other L.S.T.'s who were also taking shelter. We dropped our stern anchor and hoped. If we loose this we will put to sea.

January 6, 1944 Thursday – Tunis

We are still riding out the storm. The soldiers we have aboard and are going home are also getting burned up. At dusk we got underway then received a message to return where we were and anchored.

January 7, 1944 Friday – Bay of Tunis

The weather is easing up. We moved closer to Bizerte; but still remain in the Bay of Tunis.

Tunis and Bizerte

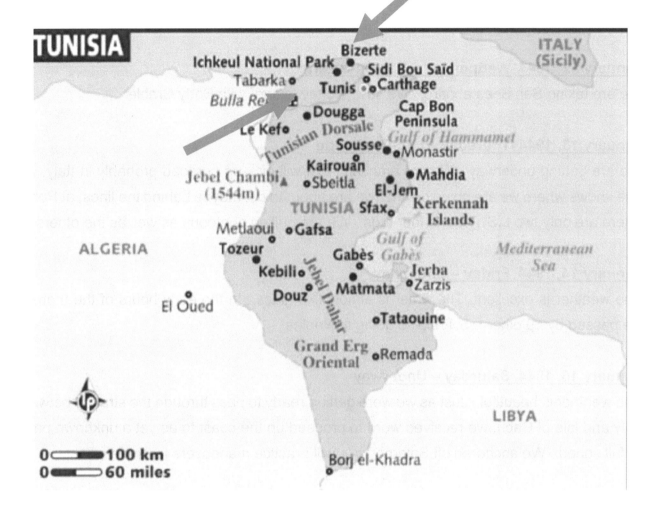

January 8, 1944 Saturday – Lac-De-Bizerte

Tied up to docks and received many letter and bulletins. We move near the Delta and had our stove fixed.

January 9, 1944 Sunday – Lac-De-Bizerte

We noticed everyone is preparing for another evasion.

January 10, 1944 Monday – Lac-De-Bizerte

We went on Liberty and saw Larry and some of his friends. We attended a box show that evening.

January 11, 1944 Tuesday – Lac-De-Bizerte

The ship next to ours caught a fire and oil on the water was also burning causing pillars of black smoke and flames. Attend box match with Kaybar. All L.S.T.'s and L.C.T. (Landing Craft Tank)'s left a couple of days ago.

January 12, 1944 Wednesday – Lac-De-Bizerte

We are taking Sea Bees aboard. We saw "Coney Island" with Betty Crable.

January 13, 1944 Thursday – Lac-De-Bizerte

We are getting underway. We are emptied. We will pick up our load probably in Italy. No one knows where we are going or what we are about to do; maybe behind the lines, at Rome. There are only two L.S.T.'s and four tugs. We are pulling pontoons as well as the others.

January 14, 1944 Friday – Underway

The weather is excellent. The water is almost like glass. In the early hours of the morning we passed by 19 other L.S.T.'s also going to Naples.

January 15, 1944, Saturday – Underway

The weather is beautiful. Just as we were getting ready to pass through the straight between Italy and Isle of Capri, we received word to proceed up the coast to as yet a unknown party, at full speed. We anchored off Salerno. We will practice maneuvers for three weeks.

January 16, 1944 Sunday – Salerno

Tied up in Salerno Harbor. Had another ship tied up #1. There is three of us L.S.T.'s together.

January 17, 1944 Monday – Salerno

We are taking British Soldiers aboard. We haven't a complete load. The men are assault troops. At sundown we moved out into the Bay of Salerno and dropped anchor.

January 18, 1944 Tuesday – Salerno

The other L.S.T. left and went on maneuvers. We are cruising about and probably join them later. We are allowed to sleep all day because we will be up all night on maneuvers. As usually there is all kinds of scuttlebutt as to where we will land; but as yet no one knows where it will be. We joined the rest by afternoon and went on maneuvers.

January 19, 1944 Wednesday – Salerno

At midnight small boats were loaded with assault troops. At 0:200 we had G.Q. (General Quarters) at which time we unloaded out ducks after closing in toward the beach and anchored. We had G.Q. for one hour, after which we retired to our sacks.

At daybreak we had a Red Naples during which time we practiced landings which turned out successful. We landed on Salerno Beach about where we did the initial invasion of Italy; but this time it was greeting Italian girls instead of German's. We made our way back to Salerno Harbor which was only a few miles away. We were granted Liberty. Within five minutes we were in the heart of Salerno. We bought Hansen and myself, a guitar and souvenirs for my Mochero, Thelm. We had a very enjoyable time. We are now ready for the invasion.

January 20, 1944 Thursday – Salerno

We are all loaded with ducks and trucks and are waiting for sailing orders. We moved out to the outer harbor late in the afternoon. We played football all afternoon which caused quite a few sore muscles. After 17.00 now, our skipper came down and told us we were going to invade the South of Rome. There is 100 "E" Boats within 50 miles and also 6 subs that they know of. Our job is to get the German 10th Army.

January 21, 1944 Friday – Underway

We are having swell weather. We had G.Q. (General Quarters) at sunrise.

January 22, 1944 Saturday – Anzio (*see map p.95*)

We arrived 23.00. We were the first ship. The M.S. cleaned the path and moved up within 2½ miles from shore. There was no action at all until our ratchet boats lasted the beach. All our small boat men returned with the last of one small boat. We discharged our ducks at 2:30. Nothing more happened until daybreak. When we had "Red Anzio". There were no enemy planes. The British war ships are blasting away at the shore. We establish the beach head within 45 minutes. We were at G.Q. all this while - all the rest of the day. We moved into closer range of the beach to discharge our equipment, but after the 88th got our range and shot at us for an hour or so we had to move out. Shrapnel flying all around us and landing all over the deck. At Sundown we got secured; but we were kept running to G.Q. all night. Enemy boats were trying to attack us but were repulsed by our ships.

January 23, 1944 Sunday – Anzio

All morning we had G.Q. (General Quarters) at 11.00 we weighted anchor once more with the hopes of getting unloaded. We waited around all day until 16:00 then we proceeded to the beach. It took us ten minutes to unload. While unloading a German tank came down on the beach and started firing at our ships. When we were pulling away from the beach we had and air attack. We moved out about ten miles. We will lay here all night to await a convoy back to Salerno.

January 24, 1944 Monday – Anzio

We pulled out early with two other L.S.T.'s and no escorts. It was fairly rough; had several air raids on the way. As we entered the vicinity of Naples we had another air raid. A smoke screen was laid down at which time we almost collided with another L.S.T. We dropped anchor and had air raids all night.

January 25, 1944 Tuesday – Pozzuoli (*see map*)

We tied up and was aloud to go ashore, in work clothes. Kaybar and myself spent all afternoon ashore at which time I bought some souvenirs. We took boxes of food to an orphanage. It is a pity in which way the people live here. We took on M-4's and by dusk we pulled out. We also received mail.

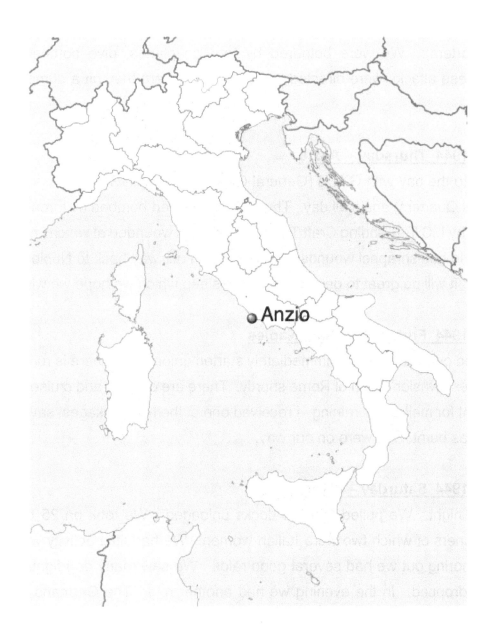

Anzio is a city and *comune* on the coast of the Lazio region of **Italy**, about 51 kilometres (32 mi) south of **Rome**.

Well known for its seaside harbour setting, it is a fishing port and a departure point for ferries and hydroplanes to the Pontine Islands of Ponza, Palmarola and Ventotene. The city bears great historical significance as the site of Operation *Shingle*, a crucial landing by the Allies during the Italian Campaign of World War II.

Wikipedia

January 26, 1944 Wednesday – Underway

We ran into very rough weather and could not enter Anzio to unload. All night we had G.Q.'s. (General Quarters). We were bothered by torpedo planes, dive bombers and regular bombers. These attacks were directed on the beach, where they hit a dump which burned for hours.

January 27, 1944 Thursday – Anzio

We moved into the bay with G.Q.'s (General Quarters) every few minutes. We finally stood G.Q. (General Quarters) again all day. The German's dived bombed us through out the day. We unloaded by L.C.T. (Landing Craft Tank) and took on wounded at which I met Young from Fox Chase. He had shrapnel wounds. We started on our way back to Naples. We all were glad to leave. It will be great to get a quiet nights sleep which we hope we will get.

January 28, 1944 Friday – Numidia Naples

We discharged our wounded and immediately started unloading. There is rumors of another behind the lines invasion North of Rome shortly. There are carriers and cruisers waiting now. When we went for mail it was raining. I received one of the two packages, saved a fruit cake. All the mail was burnt. We were on our way.

January 29, 1944 Saturday – Anzio

No raids last night. We pulled into the docks unloaded. We took on 25 trucks and 108 German prisoners of which two were Italian women. We had little activity while unloading; but after anchoring out we had several good raids. We saw many dog fights. Quite a few bombs were dropped. In the evening we had another raid. The Germans were dropping circling torpedos. They hit something off our port side which threw material high in the air, probably was an ammunition ship. We saw our fighters bag a few planes. While this raid is going on we got underway back to Naples.

No Drill This! A Nazi Shell Just Misses Army Ducks at Anzio

*Note that the Red Anzio Nazi Prisoners picture was on the front
cover of the National Geographic Magazine. The arrow is where Al is.

January 30, 1944 Sunday - Numidia Naples

We are now loading heavy guns. We learned that the Germans sunk a cruiser and Liberty ship last night at Anzio. It was tragic and received mail. Got underway to Anzio carrying more Americans for a change. We discharged our cargo and got underway at dusk. During the day we had German 200,s shooting at us; three raids. We saw the cruisers and Liberty ships that had been sunk. The Liberty ship was wrapped into a ball and was still smoking; the cruiser had sunk except for a small part of her side.

January 31, 1944 Monday – NO LOG (Thelm said Al must have been busy)

February 1, 1944 Tuesday – Baiae, Italy (*see map p.100*)

We arrived here this morning and went ashore. Bought a pair of wooden shoes. This place is dead. We loaded American troops with 90's. At sundown we pulled out. We are still having good weather.

February 2, 1944 Wednesday – Anzio

While unloading I talked with Al Mack. After a couple raids we were unloaded and underway.

February 3, 1944 Thursday – Naples

Arrived here last night.

February 4, Friday 6, Saturday 1944 – No Log

February 7, 1944 Sunday – Palermo

Because of the storm we anchored in the bay last night. Today we tied up and loaded some boxes to take to Anzio. I missed Liberty.

February 8, 1944 Monday – Palermo

Pulled out in the afternoon with nice weather toward Bizerte.

BAIAE

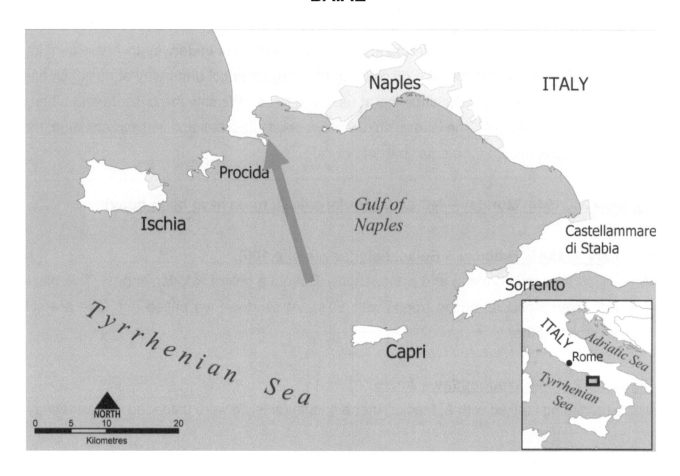

Baiae was an ancient Roman town situated on the northwest shore of the Gulf of Naples, and now in the *comune* of Bacoli. The city, which was located over natural volcanic vents, was famous for its healing medicinal hot springs which occurred all around the city and were quite easy to build spas over.

It was a fashionable resort for centuries in antiquity, particularly towards the end of the Roman Republic, when it was reckoned as superior to Pompeii, Herculaneum, and Capri by the super-rich who built luxurious villas here from 100 BC to 500 AD. It was notorious for its hedonistic offerings and the attendant rumours of corruption and scandal.

The lower part of the town later became submerged in the sea due to local volcanic, bradyseismic activity which raised or lowered the land, and recent underwater archaeology has revealed many of the fine buildings now protected in the submerged archaeological park.

February 9, 1944 Tuesday – Underway

Ran into rough weather.

February 10, 1944 Wednesday – Lac-De-Bizerte

Tied up. Saw "One Night in the Tropics" with Abbott and Costello. Received our mail.

February 11, 1944 Thursday – Lac-De-Bizerte

I received more mail. Saw "Heaven Can Wait".

February 12, 1944 Friday – Lac-De-Bizerte

Received no mail saw "Adventure in Paris" (check title)

February 13, 1944 Saturday – Lac-De-Bizerte

Received mail. Saw "Ravalli" with Beverly". Also started loading today.

February 14, 1944 Monday – Lac-De-Bizerte

We are getting underway with souvenirs and going to Arzew (see map)

February 15 & 16, 1944, – No Log Wrong Date

February 17, 1944 Thursday – Underway

Encountered bad weather and had to put into port at Philippeville.

February 18, 1944 Friday – Philippeville

Waiting for the storm to recede.

February 19, 1944 Saturday – Underway

Ran into rough weather.

February 20, 1944 Sunday – Underway

Arrived in Argew – met Geiss.

February 21, 1944 – No Log

February 22, 1944 Tuesday – Arzew (See map)

Practice loading and unloading. Received mail. Sent a rifle and a sword home and cost $0.41 cents.

February 23, 1944 Wednesday – Arzew

Received my pen and mail. Practiced maneuvers last night and again tonight.

February 24, 1944 Thursday – Arzew

We are still going on maneuvers. We go out at dusk and come in at day break.

Feb. 25, 1944 Friday – Arzew

There is no Liberty for our ship. We are going out tonight on maneuvers. We just received word that the 348 stopped to fish with the loss of 23 men and 4 officers in Anzio.

Feb. 26, 1944 Saturday – Arzew

We laid in all day and received mail.

Feb. 27, 1944 Sunday – Arzew

Sent home 2 helmets $0.24 Receive no mail. Pulled out on maneuvers at dusk.

Feb. 28, 1944 Monday – Arzew

Pulled in at dawn. Practiced loading all day.

March 1-2, 1944 Wednesday & Thursday – No Log

March 3, 1944 Friday – Underway

We got underway in a large convoy bound for Bizerte then Italy. We are traveling, with sixty ships.

March 4, 1944 Saturday – Underway

Picked up more ships at Algiers. We are having pretty good weather.

ARZEW

Arzew is a port city in **Algeria**, 25 miles (40 km) from **Oran**. It is the capital of **Arzew District**, **Oran Province**.Like the rest of North Africa, the site of modern-day Arzew was originally inhabited by the Berbers. Arzew's original Berber population came mainly from the nearby town of Bethioua, families from nearby Mostaganem, Kabyles that were deported there, as well as some semi-nomadic tribe called *Hamian*.

It was named *Arsenaria*, or *Portus Magnus* (Great Harbour) under the Roman Empire (the latter name is the one that can be seen in its former coat of arms). It has several Roman remains, mosaics, and artworks, which were removed to the museum of nearby Oran. During Roman times, Arzew's exports used to be grain and salt. The Vandals destroyed *Portus Magnus* in 429/430.

Since the Muslim conquests, it regained some importance, as it was noted by the geographer *El Bekri*, during his description of North Africa (1068) where he described the Roman ruins as *Arzao*, an abandoned Roman port. The Almohads refounded the port in 1162. Under the Ziyanids, the port, located near the Ziyanid Tlemcen was renamed to **Marsa Ben Zian** (i.e. *the port of the Zian tribe*).

Location of Arzew within Oran Province

March 5-7, 1944 Sunday-Tuesday – No Log

March 8, 1944 Wednesday – Naples

Received a little mail. On the way over spotted subs. G.Q. (General Quarters), then held morning and evening.

March 9, 1944 Thursday – Naples

Went ashore. Received no mail. The harbor is one of the biggest. Unloaded 65 ships at once. Loaded with rations and pulled out.

March 10, 1944 Friday – Angio

Arrived early and tied up and began to unload. Went on a scavenger hunt thru the city. Had two air alerts in the morning. Took all morning to unload because of the cargo. During air alerts a shell land near us. We are loading with trucks. We could watch both sides shelling one another as we left. It was been very warm and the water very smooth.

March 11, 1944 Saturday – Underway – Naples

Had 2 air alerts at morn with little attack.

March 12, 1944 Sunday – Naples

Went a shore for a few hours. Had small air raid.

March 13, 1944 Monday – Naples

Loaded up with ammunition.

March 14, 1944 Tuesday – Anzio

Arrived early. It was clear weather and we were under shell fire all day. .88 and 170's and 20's etc. While unloading Kay and myself went on another scavenger hunt. While pulling out our anchor caught another. We had to burn the anchor off and at which time the shells where hitting close, the shrapnel rained all over and some came thru in our steering room. We got underway at dusk at which time we were under an air raid.

March 15, 1944 Wednesday – Naples

Had air raid in the morning. Planes were firing within close range but no hits. Liberty was granted at 09:00. Loaded with supplies and pulled out at dusk.

March 16, 1944 Thursday – Angio

Came into Angio with air raid and also shelling of the harbor. Germans planes dropped bombs in the tacon, (Army tactical control unit or base) as we were pulling in. After tying up Kay and I left the ship and got a ride thru the City of Angio and to the outskirts of the city. Had several raids during the day. At dusk got underway and headed back to Naples.

March 17, 1944 Friday – Naples

Went on Liberty, saw "The Kings Palace and the Kings Church". Bought some souvenirs.

March 18, 1944 Saturday – Naples

Sent some more things home. Loaded up more "amo". Got underway at sunset for Angio.

March 19, 1944 Sunday – Angio

Arrived with G.Q. (General Quarters) shelling all day, couldn't leave the ship. Sounded like we were starting a push. Pulled out at dusk toward Naples.

March 20, 1944 Monday – Naples

Received mail while pulling in we hit and busted our screw and put a hole thru the bottom.

March 21, 1944 Tuesday – Naples

Laid around all day. Had G. Q. (General Quarters) at sunset. No action.

March 22, 1944 Wednesday – Naples

Mt. Vesuvius has been erupting for several days and today it is much worst. Lava is running thru the town and smoke it billowing thousands of feet into the air with occasional bursts of flames.   We got and L.C.T. (Landing Craft Tank, an amphibious assault ship for landing tanks on beachheads. Built in 1944.), to pull to Palermo and got underway at 13:00.

March 23, 1944 Thursday – No Log

March 24, 1944 Friday – Palermo

Arrived early and pulled next to Delta. Found Hayes transferred to the States.

March 25, 1944 Saturday – Palermo

Went on Liberty and bought souvenirs including a watch. Also visited the famous Catacombs.
Had Ski, Krum, and new Italian boy with me.

March 26, 1944 Sunday - Palermo

We are preparing to put four more 20's on board and another 40.

March 27, 28 1944 Monday - Tuesday – No Log

March 29, 1944 Wednesday – Palermo

Went in dry dock for repairs. Went on Liberty with Ski. Received mail.

March 30, Thursday – Palermo

Still in dry dock.

March 31, 1944 Friday – No Log

April 1, 1944 Saturday – Palermo

Still in dry dock no mail.

April 2, 3 1944 Sunday Monday – No Log

April 4, 1944 Tuesday – Palermo

In dry dock.

April 5, 1944 Wednesday – Palermo

Left dry dock received mail.

April 6, 1944 Thursday – Palermo

Had short Liberty because we got underway to Naples.

April 7, 1944 Saturday

Arrived last night. This morning pulled in and tied up.

April 8, 1944 Sunday – Easter Sunday Naples

Laid around all day. Loaded up at night and departed. Arrived at Anzio at daybreak. Went through usual shelling etc. By 14:00 we were underway again.

April 9, 1944 Monday – Naples

Arrived early and tied up.

April 11, 1944 Tuesday – Naples

Received word to detain all hands aboard, no Liberty etc. Go sailing orders for the next day. We are expecting to go to England.

April 12, 1944 Wednesday – Naples

Got underway, excellent weather toward Palermo where we are to stop and then proceed to Oran as far as we know.

April 13, 1944 Thursday – No Log

April 14, 1944 Friday – Palermo

Arrived late, no Liberty.

April 15, 1944 Saturday –Palermo

Had Liberty and took beer with us.

April 16, 1944 Sunday – Palermo

Saw friends formally from our ship on other new L.S.T.'s.

April 17, 1944 Monday – Palermo

No mail today.

April 18, 1944 Tuesday – Palermo

Pulled out at 17:00, while doing so the Biscayne whished us luck. We believe we are going to England. When outside the breakwater our convoy left us which we waited for forward orders.

April 19, 1944 Wednesday – Palermo

Went on Liberty.

April 20, 1944 Thursday – Palermo

Received mail, my camera and papers. (side note from Thelma; She said Al hinted in his letters to his mom many times for a camera but never got the hint to send him one until now.) Getting ready to pull out to Oran. Stood first watch 8-12.

April 21, 1944 Friday – Underway

By ourselves with a L.C.T. (Landing Craft Tank) and two escorts. Weather good.

April 22, 1944 Saturday – No Log

April 23, 1944 Sunday – Underway off Algeria

Past large convoy and had air coverage.

April 24, 1944 Monday – Underway

Weather still good. Arrive at Oran about 16:00 and immediately tied up to a tanker.

April 25, 1944 Tuesday – No Log

April 26, 1944 Wednesday – Oran

Made preparations for our L.C.T. (Landing Craft Tank)

April 27, 1944 Thursday – Oran

Received L.C.T. (Landing Craft Tank) went on Liberty with Ski. To cloudy to take pictures.

April 28, 29 1944 Friday, Saturday – No Log

April 30, 1944 Sunday – Oran

Got underway. The convoy is rather large. Good sailing weather.

May 1, 1944 Monday - Underway

At 23.00 we passed thru the Straight of Gibraltar

May 2-3, 1944 Tuesday, Wednesday – No Log

May 4, 1944 Thursday – Underway

We are still traveling West and as yet we don't know where we are going to land, just the United Kingdom. Weather is still good.

May 5, 1944 Friday – Underway

Still heading W/NW weather about the same.

May 6, 1944 Saturday – No Log

May 7, 1944 Sunday – Underway

Even though, our trip is about half over it is still hard to realize that we are out of the Mediterranean.   Yesterday was a little rough, but today is rather quite with the sun trying to come through the low hanging clouds.

May 8-9, 1944 Monday, Tuesday – No Log

May 10, 1944 Wednesday – Underway of France

Had sub contact at which time depth charges were dropped while we spread out.

May 11, 1944 Thursday – Underway off England

Had another sub contact. During the night debt charges were dropped. Sited England in the Afternoon. The sunsets in the region at 11:00.

May 12, 1944 Friday – England Swansea

Arrived late last night and immediately came into tie up by going through a canal with locks. Inside it was a network of canals. We unloaded our tank deck and then tied up to wait for further orders.

May 13, 1944 Saturday – England Swansea

Went on Liberty with Shi, & George. Best Liberty town yet. (Swansea is a coastal city and county in Wales).

May 14, 1944 Sunday – Mother's Day Swansea

We pulled out and headed for Plymouth where we will unload our L.C.T (Landing Craft Tank).

May 15, 1944 Monday – English Channel

Had a sub contact early morning. Plymouth just had air raid at which time radio bombs were used.

May 16, 1944 Tuesday – Plymouth

Saw a movie with Geo. Browns in "1st. Next To Go".

May 17, 1944 Wednesday – Plymouth

Went on working party which turned out to be nothing more than a Liberty Party in the Arsenal. Received more mail. Took L.C.T. (Landing Craft Tank) off.

May 18, 1944 Thursday – Plymouth

Spent most of the day writing letters and walked around the yard.

May 19, 1944 Friday – Plymouth

Went on Liberty and saw "Captain Courageous". Weather was excellent.

May 20–23, 1944 Saturday – Tuesday – No Log

May 24, 1944 Wednesday – Plymouth

Loaded some fancy provisions and moved out of harbor.

May 25, 1944 Thursday – Plymouth

We are still lying around because of our crew being missing due to failure to find the ship. We are making all arrangements for the coming invasions.

May 26-28, 1944 Friday – Sunday – No Log

May 29, 1944 Monday – Plymouth

Early this morning we had air alert consisting of only recognizance Plane.

May 30, 1944 Tuesday – No Log

May 31, 1944 Wednesday – Plymouth

Received gas outfits. Some L.S.T.'s have already loaded.

June 1, 1944 Thursday – Plymouth

Made 2/6. We moved to the other side of the harbor.

June 2, 1944 Friday – Plymouth

At midnight we began loading with mostly jugs carrying gas and oil. Got underway at daybreak and headed up the coast. We will rendezvous with a very large convoy. As yet we do not know what "H" is for or "D Day" are.

June 3, 1944 Saturday – Slocomb

Arrived at a little town opposite our objective.

June 4, 1944 Sunday – Slocomb

Still waiting to sail. We received mail.

June 5, 1944 Monday – Solcombe

We left late in the afternoon to form with the other convoy. As soon as we left we had to wear our gas outfits at all times. (Solcombe is a seaside town in the South Hams district of Devon, south west England noted for boating and shipbuilding/sailing port.)

June 6-9, 1944 Tuesday-Friday – No Log

June 10, 1944 Saturday – Underway

Back in England in Portland. We brought back ninety wounded. Some air borne troops, others from the L.S.T. 999 which was sank by a mine. Many ships were sunk by mines. We had over 800 German Prisoners which we transferred to another ship. We had very little trouble and very few air alerts.

June 11, 1944 Sunday – Portland

Arrived and discharged our wounded and loaded up with Engineers.

June 12, 1944 Monday – Underway

We moved out very early. Arrived 22.00 and unloaded. We are beaching tomorrow. The tide is in only one and a half hours.

June 13, 1944 Tuesday – France

Instead of beaching we unloaded our platoons. It is now 19.00 and we are underway to England.

June 14, 1944 Wednesday – England Portland

We received a little mail. Waiting to load up again and pull out. (Portland is a peninsula of the English Channel coast, southern England.

June 15, 1944 Thursday – No Log

June 16, 1944 Friday – Underway

Arrived in France and we are beaching as soon as the tide rises. There is no action taking place over here.

June 17, 1944 Saturday – France

Unloaded and laid around all day. From 12-4 we had from 5-6 raids at which time enemy planes dropped bombs rather close. We could see both sides taking action. First German Ack-Ack (anti-aircraft artillery), then ours.

June 18, 1944 Sunday – France and Underway

Got underway early. One troop ship coming with us struck a mine off the beach head and we left her.

June 19, 1944 Monday – England

Loaded and got underway. Received 1 letter from Thelm.

June 20, 1944 Tuesday – Underway

Almost to France we turned around and headed for England. Past two more convoy's with L.S.T. (Americans) turning around. In the evening we landed at South Hampton to await the passing of a storm nearby.

June 21, 1944 Wednesday – Spit Head, England (Isle of Wight & Hampshire Point)

Still laying around, waiting for the gale to die out.

June 22, 23 1944 Thursday, Friday – No Log

June 24, 1944 Saturday – South Hampton

Loaded up and got underway, but missed our convoy and returned to South Hampton to await for more sailing orders.

June 25, 1944 Sunday – South Hampton

Missed another convoy.

June 26, 1944 Monday – South Hampton

Missed another convoy. During the night and early morning some robot planes flew over and even dropped nearby. Pulled out early.

OMAHA BEACH FRANCE

June 27, 1944 Tuesday – France

Arrived late. Several attempts we landed and got unloaded.

June 28, 29 1944 Wednesday, Thursday – No Log

June 30, 1944 Friday – England

Arrived back and loaded late at night.

July 1, 1944 Sunday – England

Left for France and arrived late.

July 2, 1944 Saturday, Sunday – No Log

July 3, 1944 Monday – England

Arrived back in England late.

July 4, 1944 Tuesday – England

Went ashore with Ray while the ship was unloading. Received some more mail. Brought back 700 Germans at which time I got some German belts.

July 5, 1944 Wednesday – France

Arrive early and started to discharge our cargo. Late at night pulled off the beach.

July 6, 1944 Thursday – England

Arrived and loaded

HISTORY

JUNE 06, 1944 : D-DAY

Although the term D-Day is used routinely as military lingo for the day an operation or event will take place, for many it is also synonymous with June 6, 1944, the day the Allied powers crossed the English Channel and landed on the beaches of Normandy, France, beginning the liberation of Western Europe from Nazi control during World War II. Within three months, the northern part of France would be freed and the invasion force would be preparing to enter Germany, where they would meet up with Soviet forces moving in from the east.

With Hitler's armies in control of most of mainland Europe, the Allies knew that a successful invasion of the continent was central to winning the war. Hitler knew this too, and was expecting an assault on northwestern Europe in the spring of 1944. He hoped to repel the Allies from the coast with a strong counterattack that would delay future invasion attempts, giving him time to throw the majority of his forces into defeating the Soviet Union in the east. Once that was accomplished, he believed an all-out victory would soon be his.

On the morning of June 5, 1944, U.S. General Dwight D. Eisenhower, the supreme commander of Allied forces in Europe gave the go-ahead for Operation Overlord, the largest amphibious military operation in history. On his orders, 6,000 landing craft, ships and other vessels carrying 176,000 troops began to leave England for the trip to France. That night, 822 aircraft filled with parachutists headed for drop zones in Normandy. An additional 13,000 aircraft were mobilized to provide air cover and support for the invasion.

By dawn on June 6, 18,000 parachutists were already on the ground; the land invasions began at 6:30 a.m. The British and Canadians overcame light opposition to capture Gold, Juno and Sword beaches; so did the Americans at Utah. The task was much tougher at Omaha beach, however, where 2,000 troops were lost and it was only through the tenacity and quick-wittedness of troops on the ground that the objective was achieved. By day's end, 155,000 Allied troops–Americans, British and Canadians–had successfully stormed Normandy's beaches.

For their part, the Germans suffered from confusion in the ranks and the absence of celebrated commander Field Marshal Erwin Rommel, who was away on leave. At first, Hitler, believing that the invasion was a feint designed to distract the Germans from a coming attack north of the Seine River, refused to release nearby divisions to join the counterattack and reinforcements had to be called from further afield, causing delays. He also hesitated in calling for armored divisions to help in the defense. In addition, the Germans were hampered by effective Allied air support, which took out many key bridges and forced the Germans to take long detours, as well as efficient Allied naval support, which helped protect advancing Allied troops.

Though it did not go off exactly as planned, as later claimed by British Field Marshal Bernard Montgomery–for example, the Allies were able to land only fractions of the supplies and vehicles they had intended in France–D-Day was a decided success. By the end of June, the Allies had 850,000 men and 150,000 vehicles in Normandy and were poised to continue their march across Europe.

The heroism and bravery displayed by troops from the Allied countries on D-Day has served as inspiration for several films, most famously *The Longest Day* (1962) and *Saving Private Ryan* (1998). It was also depicted in the HBO mini-series *Band of Brothers* (2001).

Isle of Wight

July 7, 1944 Friday – England

Awaited sailing orders

July 8, 1944 Saturday – France Courseulles (Courseulles-sur-Mer, a village)

While awaiting for the tide we,   Ski and I went for a walk to Counselees. At night we had and air raid at which time few bombs were dropped. Strafing was done mostly. Saw quite a bit ack.ack, (anti-aircraft artillery).

July 9, 1944 Sunday – Underway off France

Got underway early for a town next to London.

July 10, 1944 Monday – England, London

Had Liberty from 13.00 – 10.00.

July 12, 1944 Wednesday – England underway

Left England for France

July 13, 1944 – No Log

July 14, 1944 Friday – France

Unloaded and went ashore. Visited a French summer resort. At night had an airraid. No bombs.

July 15, 1944 Saturday – France

At night had another air attack. Not much strength. Headed back to England and got lost in a fog bank. Liberty ship collided with us and other ships through out the fog almost did.

July 16, 1944 Sunday – Off England

Still in a heavy fog. We anchored to a wait clearing to see where we are.

July 17, 1944 Monday

Still in fog bank. Got another box to send home.

July 18, 1944 Tuesday – England

Fog cleared and we moved up the Tames to tie up and get some repairs. We are in Tilbury. (See map)

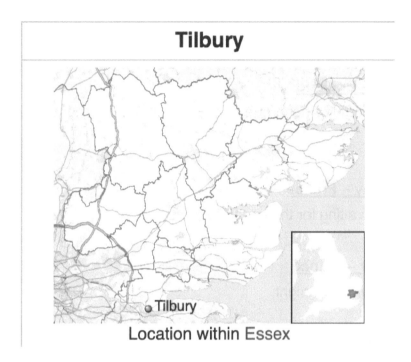

Tilbury

Location within Essex

July 19, 1944 Wednesday – England

Went on Liberty and spent it in a small town called Grays. "The Doodle Boys" come over all night long.

July 20, 1944 Thursday – England

Got raided

July 21, 1944 Friday – England underway

Left in the afternoon for France

July 22, 1944 Sunday – France

Anchored with delayed order because of bad weather.

July 23, 1944 Sunday – France

Had several small air raids

July 24, 1944 Monday – France underway

Left France arrived in England early the next morning.

July 26, 1944 Wednesday – England

Received a little mail. No Liberty as usual. Box finally left the ship.

July 28, 1944 Friday – England

Loaded up and moved out to Anchorage. Did nothing but tried to get repairs. Received more mail.

July 29, 1944 Saturday – France

Beached at 19:00 are waiting for the tide to run out.

July 30, 1944 Sunday – France

Unloaded today. No raids last night.

July 31, 1944 Monday – France

Went from beach to beach trying to get a convoy to the Thames.

August 1, 1944 Tuesday – Underway to England

August 2, 1944 Wednesday – No Log

August 3, 1944 Thursday – London England

Received 48 and went to hospital for glasses.

August 4-9, 1944 Friday - Wednesday – No Log

August 10, 1944 Thursday – London England

After doing minor repairs we loaded up and this is to be our last trip from London.

August 11, 1944 Friday – France - Gold Beach

We have to go back to Plymouth for major overhaul and then we are all hoping some of us will get transferred. We are having unusual weather very good.

August 12, 1944 Saturday – No Log

August 13, 1944 Sunday – England, Plymouth

We are getting major overhauls.

August 14, 1944 Monday – No Log

August 15, 1944 Tuesday – England, Plymouth

We are getting major overhauls. Had Liberty. Received glasses and mail.

August 16, 1944 Wednesday – England, Plymouth

The good weather has been broken and we are back to normal, cloudy.

August 17, 1944 Thursday – England, Plymouth

Had Liberty. Received mail.

August 18, 1944 Friday – England, Plymouth

August 19, 20 1944 Saturday, Sunday – No Log

August 21, 1944 Monday – Plymouth

Been ashore last few days and had Liberty yesterday with a 48 tomorrow. Been receiving mail quite regular.

August 22, 1944 Tuesday – Plymouth

Went on a 48 to Torquay. (See map p.122; a seaside town in Devon England). Had excellent time.

August 23, 1944 Wednesday – No Log

August 24, 1944 Thursday – Plymouth

Had Liberty just went to shows.

August 25-26, 1944 Friday, Saturday – No Log

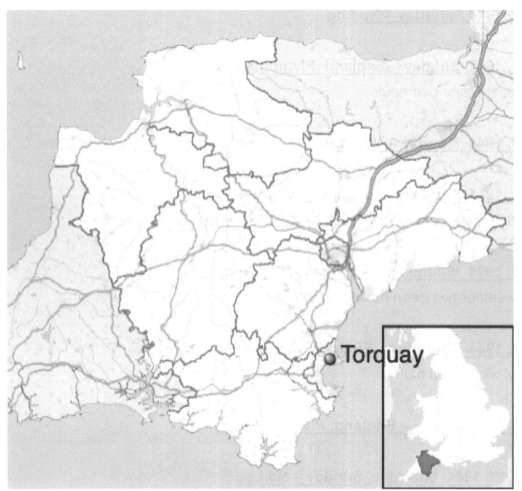

Location within Devon

August 27, 1944 Sunday – Southampton

We are getting 5 day leave.

August 28, 1944 Monday – No Log

August 29, 1944 Tuesday – Southampton

Went on Liberty saw "Two Girls and a Sailor". Received a little mail.

August 30-31, 1944 Wednesday, Thursday – No Log

September 1, 1944 Friday – Underway

Loaded small supplies.

September 2, 1944 Saturday – St. Michael

Had bad weather, it will take seven days to unload.

September 4, 1944 Monday – St. Michael

Bad weather made us stay at anchor.

September 5, 1944 Tuesday – Underway

Arrived in England, Southampton and received some mail. While in St. Michael got a new camera.

September 6-8, 1944 Wednesday, Thursday, Friday – No Log

September 9, 1944 Saturday – Southampton

First draft left the ship for the states. We loaded up and pulled out in the harbor. (Twenty-one men)

September 10, 1944 Sunday – Southampton

Still waiting on sailing orders.

September 11, 1944 Monday – Southampton

Still waiting for sailing orders. Had my five days moved back.

September 12, 1944 Tuesday - Southampton – No Log

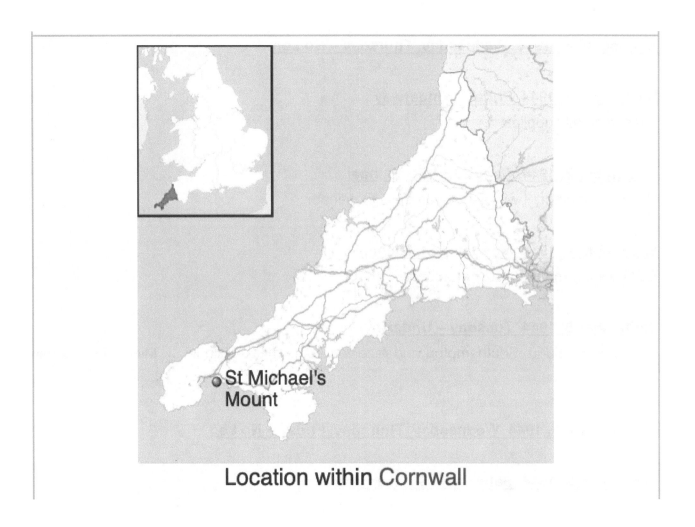

Location within Cornwall

September 13, 1944 Wednesday– St. Michael

Arrived at St. Michael was nice weather. (See map; a small island in Mt. Bay in the UK) We expect another draft when we get back.

September 14, 15, 1944 Thursday, Friday – No Log

September 16, 1944 Saturday – Southampton

Arrived back and received some mail.

September 17, 1944 Sunday – Southampton

Took pictures of Engineers.

124

September 18, 1944 Monday – Underway

While underway we ran into another L.S.T putting a hole in our Starboard side. Passed Cherbourg on the way to the beach.

September 19, 20, 1944 Tuesday, Wednesday – No Log

September 21, 1944 Thursday – France

We unloaded and waiting for sailing orders.

September 22, 1944 Friday – No Log

September 23, 1944 Saturday – Southampton

Had Liberty and spent it with Kay and Johnson in Shirley.

September 24, 1944 Sunday – Southampton

Loaded up and moved to outer anchorage. We have taken on supplies of oil and have orders for others, so we believe we will take our ship back to the states soon.

September 25-30, 1944 Monday-Saturday – No Log

October 1, 2 1944 Sunday, Monday – No Log

October 3, 1944 Tuesday – Southampton

Returned from our five day leave which I spent in London. Went on Liberty the same day in Southampton.

October 4, 1944 Wednesday

Loaded up and moved out to outer anchorage. There is more talk of returning to the States but as yet nothing definite yet.

October 5 – 12, 1944 Thursday-Thursday – No Log

October 13, 1944 Friday– Southampton

Arrived back after being in France riding out a storm and trying to get unloaded.

October 14–21, 1944 Saturday - Saturday – No Log

October 22, 1944 Sunday– Plymouth England

Arrived here for repairs.

October 23 – November 1, 1944 Monday-Wednesday – No Log

November 2, 1944 Thursday – Plymouth England

Just came off a seventy-two leave which Johnson and I spent in London

November 3-10, 1944 Friday-Friday – No Log

November 11, 1944 Saturday – Plymouth England

Still getting repairs.

November 12, 13, 1944 Sunday, Monday – No Log

November 14, 1944 Tuesday – Plymouth England

Had 48 hour pass.

November 15-17 1944 Wednesday-Friday – No Log

November 18, 1944 Saturday – Plymouth England

Have a 48 today. Our mail situation cleared up some what.

November 19-24, 1944 Sunday-Friday – No Log

November 25, 1944 Saturday – Plymouth England

We are squaring away our ship to turn it over to the English. We turned in all our foul weather gear. As yet we don't know where and when we will turn it over, however it won't be long, maybe it will be in time to get us home for Christmas. We have been having Liberty every other night and of course with the rain to accompany us.

November 26-29, 1944 Sunday-Wednesday – No Log

November 30, 1944 Thursday – Plymouth England

We are still waiting on orders. We are suppose to be in Scotland, by the 4th which mean will be probably leave tomorrow. We still might make it by Christmas.

December 1, 1944 Friday – No Log

December 2, 1944 Saturday – Plymouth England

Left at noon for Scotland with fair weather. Ran into bad weather. Split several seams including some in fuel tanks. Late at night on the 3rd we came close to Milford Heaven where we were to put the storm out but engines stopped because of salt water in the tanks. We dropped anchor and proceeded to pump lines. After that was completed we pulled into the harbor, and after dropping anchor a half sunken freighter broke loose and came at us. We had G.Q. (General Quarters) and fortunately got underway, causing no damage.

December 3, 1944 Sunday – No Log

December 4, 1944 Monday – Zilfred Heaven Scotland

Still waiting on the storm. As yet we don't know to what extent our damage is. About all our tanks, except one is filled with salt water.

December 5, 1944 Tuesday – No Log

December 6, 1944 Wednesday – Helensburgh, Scotland

Arrived here at big Naval Base. Because of the delay caused the storm we will not decommission our ship tomorrow as planned but will wait until the 12th of December. (See map p.128; a town in Scotland that lies on the north shore.)

December 7, 1944 Thursday – Helensburgh, Scotland

There is nice scenery around here. There are snow covered mountains all around and it is quite beautiful. English came aboard today to get acquainted with the ship. They will stay aboard now and rest will come later.

December 8, 1944 Friday – Helensburgh, Scotland

Took us all our extra food today.

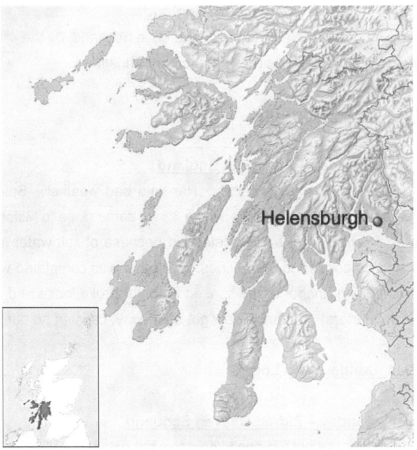

Location within Argyll and Bute

December 9, 1944 Saturday – Helensburgh, Scotland

Other L.S.T's are commissioned their ships and we are the only one left. We took aboard other fellows from the L.S.T. and they will wait on us and we will move out together, at which time we are suppose to board a liner.

December 9, 1944 Saturday – Rosenthal, Scotland (entered again)

Still waiting to decommission our ship. On the eight had Liberty in Glasgow.

December 10, 1944 Sunday – Rosenthal, Scotland

Had Liberty in Glasgow again and seen "Great American Broadcast". We are to leave tomorrow and as yet we have no further orders as for getting home for Christmas. We might stay on the beach for a couple of weeks.

December 11, 1944 Monday – Rosenthal, Scotland

Nothing new just packing.

December 12, 1944 Tuesday – Rosenthal, Scotland

Decommissioned our ship at 1300 and prepared to leave the ship at 15.00. English took over and we departed for the base. We arrived and was put in Hut 13-11. After unpacking we had chow which was good and later we attended a show. We as yet don't know when we will leave for the States.

December 13, 1944 Wednesday – Rosenthal - Base, Scotland

Did very little today. Went' to a show at night.

December 14, 1944 Thursday – Rosenthal - Base, Scotland

Had bad weather all day. Went to a show at night and saw "The Man in the Iron Mask".

December 15, 1944 Friday – Rosenthal - Base, Scotland

Weather bad all day except for a few hours. Went aboard our ship to see some of our English friends. Our names were posted to leave for the States the 17th may go back on the Wakefield.

December 16, 1944 Saturday – Rosenthal - Base, Scotland

Received our sailing orders we will leave tomorrow night. Our gear leaves us tomorrow early. Went to a show this evening and came back and backed.

December 17, 1944 Sunday – Rosenthal - Base, Scotland

We have been having wet weather all the time. This morning we shipped our gear off and will follow tonight at 23.00. At 20.00 we left by truck. Took us to the railway station at Helensburg. The train left at 24.30.

December 18, 1944 Monday – Liverpool, Scotland

Arrived at 11:00 and boarded the Mt. Vernon.

December 19, 1944 Tuesday – Liverpool Scotland

The chow we are getting is very good and isn't to many aboard which makes it a lot easier.

Shown within Merseyside

Prologue

Even though there were no more entries, Al arrived home December 24, 1944 surprising Thelma, family and friends. Later they had a big surprise party for him where he got engaged to Thelma. He was married over 50 years and lived in Moorestown, NJ and had one child, Donna. Al is survived by his daughter, Donna, son-in-law, Henry, 2 grandsons, Tony and Scott and great grandson, Mikael.

Al's passion for life included, many hobbies such as photography and computers. He continued this passion throughout his life, along with an incredible zest for knowledge, he never could get enough. If you asked him how he was feeling he would always tell you..... "never better".

Al was also very proud of both of his grandsons, who he referred to them my Number 1 grandson, Tony, and number 2 grandson, Scott. He loved their passion for life and loved when they called him for advice. He could spend a long time on the phone answering their questions and many hours, with various day trips, lunches and shared his knowledge and values to live by.

Unfortunately, Thelm passed Nov. 6, 2011 before this diary could be completed.
We all miss him so much, and thank him for all the memories and knowledge he gave each one of us over the years. We love you dad.

APPENDIX A

Turning L.S.T. 351 over to the English 12/12/44

LST-351

LST-351 was laid down on 9 November 1942 at the Norfolk Navy Yard; launched on 7 February 1943; sponsored by Mrs. P. F. Wakeman; and commissioned on 24 February 1943.

During World War II, LST-351 was assigned to the European theater and participated in the following operations:

Sicilian occupation—July 1943

Salerno landings—September 1943

Anzio-Nettuno advanced landings — January through March 1944

Invasion of Normandy—June 1944

On 12 December 1944, she was transferred to the United Kingdom. The tank landing ship was struck from the Navy list on 15 October 1946 and returned to United States Navy custody on 10 December 1946. She was sold to the Netherlands sometime between 30 December 1946 and 17 June 1947.

LST-351 earned four battle stars for World War II service.

THELM SENT THIS PICTURE TO AL

AL, LEAVING HIS SHIP

LIBERTY

1/19/45

1/25/45

135

THEM AND AL

Hawaii

THEL & Al.'

Tough Duty

APPENDIX B

U. S. S. ATLANTA (CL104)

1 December 1945.

TO WHOM IT MAY CONCERN:

Subject: ALBERT E. KLUMPP, MM1c, V6, USNR.

　　　1.   Albert E. Klumpp has served aboard the U.S.S. ATLANTA for ten (10) months as a shop machinist.

　　　2.   His attention to duty, knowledge of machine shop work and loyalty have been above average.

　　　3.   I recommend him to who ever may need his services.

                                    G. T. ELLIOTT,
                            Lieut.- Comdr., U.S.Navy,
                            Engineer Officer.

HONORARY MEMBERSHIP CARD

. No.: __1609__

Dues: XXXXX

This is to certify that
Mrs. Thelma Klumpp
is a member in good standing of
USS ATLANTA (CL104) REUNION ASSN.

TREASURER   C. Foster PRESIDENT

__Thelma Klumpp__

is a member in good standing of the
USS Atlanta Reunion Association
For the Years 2007 & 2008

B. Merrill, Pres.   C. Smith, Secy.   J. DeKorne, Trea.

TRANSMITTAL OF AND/OR ENTITLEMENT TO AWARDS

			DATE *July 28 1978*
NAME *Stumpp, Albert E.*		SERVICE NO./SSN *6514721*	BRANCH OF SERVICE *Navy*
DATE OF INQUIRY	RECEIVED ON	ON BEHALF OF	
REFERRED BY			

☐ The records show that the person named above is entitled to the following medals.
☒ The following medals authorized for issuance are enclosed.

	OAK LEAF CLUSTER		
	BRONZE	SILVER	☒ AMERICAN CAMPAIGN MEDAL (Note 1)
DISTINGUISHED FLYING CROSS			☒ ASIATIC-PACIFIC CAMPAIGN MEDAL (Note 1)
BRONZE STAR MEDAL			☒ EUROPEAN-AFRICAN-MIDDLE EASTERN CAMPAIGN MEDAL (Note 1)
____ W/LETTER "V" DEVICE			☒ WW II VICTORY MEDAL
AIR MEDAL			ARMY OF OCCUPATION MEDAL WITH ____ GERMANY ____ JAPAN CLASP
PURPLE HEART			____ BERLIN AIRLIFT DEVICE
			NAVY OCCUPATION MEDAL ____ EUROPE ____ ASIA CLASP
			NATIONAL DEFENSE SERVICE MEDAL (Note 1)
DISTINGUISHED UNIT CITATION			KOREAN SERVICE MEDAL (Note 1)
AF LONGEVITY SERVICE AWARD RIBBON			UNITED NATIONS SERVICE MEDAL
AF OUTSTANDING UNIT AWARD			VIETNAM SERVICE MEDAL (Note 1)
PRESIDENTIAL UNIT CITATION			CHINA SERVICE MEDAL (Extended)
			ARMED FORCES RESERVE MEDAL WITH ____ HOUR GLASS DEVICE(S)
			NAVAL RESERVE MEDAL
			ORGANIZED MARINE CORPS RESERVE MEDAL
NAVY UNIT COMMENDATION			MARINE CORPS RESERVE RIBBON
			EXPEDITIONARY MEDAL (Note 1)
			____ ARMED FORCES ____ MARINE CORPS ____ NAVY
☒ GOOD CONDUCT MEDAL ____ AIR FORCE ____ ARMY (Note 3)			GOLD STAR LAPEL BUTTON ____ PIN ____ CLUTCH
____ COAST GUARD ____ MARINE CORPS ☒ NAVY			____ PRESIDENTIAL UNIT CITATION (Note 2)
LOOPS: ____ BRONZE ____ SILVER			REPUBLIC OF VIETNAM CAMPAIGN MEDAL (Note 2)
STARS: ____ BRONZE ____ SILVER (Note 1)			PHILIPPINE _____ RIBBON (Note 1)
OAK LEAF CLUSTER:			☒ *Honorable Discharge Lapel Button (Ruptured Duck)*
AMERICAN DEFENSE SERVICE MEDAL WITH ____ FLEET CLASP			
____ BASE CLASP ____ BRONZE LETTER "A" (Note 1)			
____ FOREIGN SERVICE CLASP			

NOTE: 1. Ribbons, clasps and/or stars for these awards are not issued by this center but may be purchased from stores which sell military supplies.

2. This is an award of the Philippine/Korean/Vietnam government and is not issued by the United States government. They may be purchased from stores which sell military supplies.

3. Air Force enlisted personnel who qualified for the award of the Good Conduct Medal on or before May 31, 1963, are awarded the Army Good Conduct Medal. The Air Force Good Conduct Medal is awarded for qualifying service completed on or after June 1, 1963. Since the above named person qualified for the Good Conduct Medal before June 1, 1963, he is entitled only to the Army Good Conduct Medal.

☒ MEDALS THAT HAVE BEEN PREVIOUSLY ISSUED ARE INDICATED BY AN ASTERISK.

Copies of Invasions that you participated in are attached. No other information in record regarding commendation from the Navy Department.

Ralph W. McCann
Chief, Navy Reference Branch
NATIONAL PERSONNEL RECORDS CENTER
(Military Personnel Records)
9700 Page Boulevard
St. Louis, Missouri 63132

ENCLOSURE

GENERAL SERVICES ADMINISTRATION   ☆U.S. GPO: 1977-765-090/3042 Region No. 6   GSA FORM 6994 (REV. 11/77)

INVASION OF ITALY
RED BEACH, SALERNO
July 10, 1943

Name **KLUMPP, Albert E.**
(Name in Full, Surname to the Left)

651-47-21 Rate **F1c**
(Service No.)

Date Reported Aboard: **29 March 1943**

U.S.S. LST 351
(Present Ship or Station)

ATB Solomons, Md.
(Ship or Station Received From)

As a member of the crew, participated
in the invasion of Sicily, at Yellow
Beach, Licata, on July 10, 1943

L. Emley

L. Emley
Executive Officer.

- -

As a member of the crew, participated
in the invasion of Italy, at Red Beach,
Salerno, on September 10, 1943.

L. Emley

L. Emley
Executive Officer.

INVASION OF ITALY
RED BEACH, PETER SECTOR, ANZIO ITALY
January 22, 1944

Name **KLUMPP, Albert E.**
(Name in Full, Surname to the Left)

651-47-21   Rate   MM3/c
(Service No.)

Date Reported Aboard   March 29, 1943.

U.S.S. LST 351
(Present Ship or Station)

ATB Solomans, Maryland.
(Ship or Station Received From)

As a member of the crew, participated in the invasion of Italy, at Red Beach, Peter Sector, Anzio, Italy, on January 22, 1944.

L. Emley
Executive Officer.

MERITORIOUS SERVICE
HANDLING OF CASUALTIES
UTAH BEACH, FRANCE
June 8, 1944

Name **KLUMPP, Albert E.**
(Name in Full, Surname to the Left)

651-47-21   Rate **MM2/c**
(Service No.)

Date Reported Aboard: **29 March 1943**

U.S.S. LST 351
(Present Ship or Station)

ATB Solomans, Md.
(Ship or Station Received From)

Participated in the invasion of France, June 6, 1944, as a part of Force Uncle, discharging troops and equipment on the Utah Beach sector.

- -

Especially commended for meritorious service in the handling of casualties from Utah Beach, France, the night of June 8, 1944.

Richard W. Caldwell
LT. RICHARD W. CALDWELL, USNR.

Vol. LXXXVI, No. 1   WASHINGTON   July, 1944

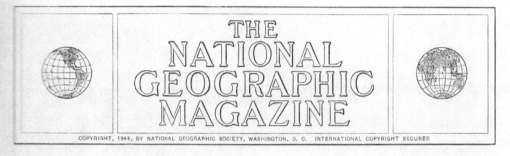

COPYRIGHT, 1944, BY NATIONAL GEOGRAPHIC SOCIETY, WASHINGTON, D. C.   INTERNATIONAL COPYRIGHT SECURED

Landing Craft for Invasion

By Melville Bell Grosvenor

YOUR soldier son, was he one of the first to land at Salerno? Or did he leapfrog up the New Guinea coast to take the Japanese by surprise at Hollandia?

Your husband, your brother, your boy friend—even your father—was he one of those gallant Marines who swarmed ashore on Kwajalein or Eniwetok in the Marshalls?

If so, he was put ashore by the men who man the landing craft of the Amphibious Force of the U. S. Navy and Coast Guard.

His huge tanks, artillery, trucks, ammunition and supplies—even his hospital staff and nurses—all were landed by the assorted craft of this important new branch of the Navy.

Like huge whales casting up thousands of Jonahs, LSTs, LCI(L)s, and LCTs and myriad small craft nose ashore and disgorge from jawlike bows the divisions and materiel that are winning battles everywhere.

Xerxes drove his Persian hordes across the Hellespont on galley bridges to attack Greece. William the Conqueror ferried his Normans across the English Channel in boats to invade the British Isles. Even the Japs have used small barges in this war. But no power has yet employed landing ships and craft on the grand scale that we are using them today.

As I write, fleets of these landing vessels jam British harbors and rivers, poised for "D" Day, ready to swarm across to "Fortress Europe," ferrying our invasion forces.

For six weeks I have been the guest of the Alligator Navy, as "Amphibs" call their outfit. Officers and men put me through a rigid course, just as they would any "boot," from knot tying to beaching.

I sat in on training classes; talked with veterans of Europe and the Pacific; bounced around in an LCI(L) in the Atlantic; and rode the ramp of a charging LST.

"It's a strange Navy, this new Amphibious Force," an old-timer told me. "All my life I have been taught to keep my ship off the reefs. Now I must steer full speed through the surf and hit the beach like a charging bull. What's more, I must keep her pinned there solidly, so the Army and its tanks can swarm ashore. Then I back off quickly and scram out of there."

No wonder Amphibs affectionately refer to their branch as the "Ambiguous Navy."

Amphibs Trained at Solomons Island

"Where do you train the thousands of officers and men needed for landing craft? Are they put aboard commissioned ships, or do they go to school first?" I asked.

"Come down to Solomons Island, on the Patuxent, and we'll show you," he replied. "You know, the Marines who took Guadalcanal in the Solomon Islands trained at Solomons Island, Maryland! And the landing crews who put them ashore learned the know-how on the Chesapeake, too."

So on a cold, blustery day I reported "aboard" the Amphibious Training Base at Solomons, Maryland. Comdr. Neill Phillips, USN, the training officer and a veteran of 22 months fighting Japs in the Pacific, was just leaving his office to welcome a new class of officers.

"Come along," he said, "and we'll put you through the works."

Along with 300 young officers, whose gold stripes still glistened, we filed into a big frame hall.

"Gentlemen, you have come here straight from civilian life and are being plunged into the center of a great historic event. Never before has a warring power developed amphibious operations—that is, the landing of an

Down the Ramp and through the Surf Goes a Half-drowned Jeep at Cape Gloucester

Marines must work fast, for Jap snipers still are active in the trees of this New Britain beachhead. LSTs (Landing Ship, Tank) bumped hard on an offshore sand bar coming in for this landing, yet Coast Guard and Navy skippers drove their ships in at full speed on schedule. The man on the bow door is taking a short cut from the forecastle to the ramp.

army from boats on an enemy's shore—to the extent the United Nations are doing today.

"Wherever the war takes us, whether it be the coasts of Europe or the Japanese islands, we must have landing craft—tens of thousands of them—to put our troops on the beaches and keep them there.

"This is *our* secret weapon!

"To man these vessels we shall need 140,000 new officers and men in the next six months. Think of that! There were only 90,000 in the whole Navy a few years ago.

"Just as we build landing craft on assembly lines, so we must train you men by mass production.

"But you do have one advantage. Because this amphib game is so new, you stand on an equal footing with us old-timers. We know very little more about it than you do. You have a chance to grow up with this child prodigy of the Navy."

Afterwards, Commander Phillips showed us

through big school buildings which buzzed with Navy talk and men filing to and from classes. I watched officers learning to tie knots and read signals, studying seamanship and navigation. Sailors fresh from farm and city were being taught to wire splice.

"Some day, knowing how to splice wire may save them from an ugly situation," the instructor said. "Towlines and stern anchor cables frequently part at awkward moments."

In one room a group was calling out the nicknames of Jap planes as the instructor flashed pictures on a screen.

"Flash drill in aircraft recognition is vital," the lieutenant said. "Officers and men must recognize planes instantly or they may shoot down friends or let enemies get away. We stress particularly six United States carrier planes.

"We begin by flashing pictures for 1/10 of a second and work up gradually to 1/75. Men impress the image on the mind and call

Up "The Slot" Two LSTs Steam, Bound for Rendova, Central Solomons

Soon these Marines are to land their heavy guns and equipment on Rendova and blast the Japanese on Munda Point. The chimneylike ventilators draw carbon-monoxide fumes from the tank deck below when tanks warm up and chug off the ship. Months of preparation went into the plans for this campaign. "The Slot" is the sailors' name for the narrow northwest passage through the Solomon Islands.

out 'Zeke' for Jap Zero, 'Janice' for JU 88, or 'Mike' for Messerschmitt 109E faster than you can say Jack Robinson.

"Also, we instruct the officers and men in dark adjustment. They must wear red goggles or remain in the dark 20 minutes to a half hour before going on night watch, so they'll have cats' eyes. We teach them how to scan, or keep the eyes moving constantly to spot objects in the darkness."

On one big field I saw two lines of sailors throwing ropes as if trying to lasso each other.

"That's our mooring school where we teach the deck forces to heave lines," the officer in charge explained. "The field is laid out like a dummy ship approaching a dummy dock. The wooden posts you see represent bitts on a ship and bollards on a dock to which the ship's lines are made fast."

I watched sailors on the "ship" throw heaving lines across the dusty "water." Men on the "dock" pulled them in, dragging across

big mooring hawsers which they carefully made fast to the posts.

In machine shops officers and sailors of the engineering department were busy tearing down and assembling every kind of amphibious motor and engine.

"We repair all our training craft here," my guide said. "In that way engineers learn practical lessons which will stand them in good stead later.

"Most of our machinists were automobile or boat mechanics in civil life. That young ensign in coveralls was engineer of a tuna-fishing boat on the west coast. This man took care of Diesels on a streamliner. He is invaluable."

On a bank overlooking the harbor, a black tank belched fire and smoke. Three rain-coated figures held a long hose, its nozzle spraying an umbrella of white mist. Above the roar of burning oil, the officer in charge was shouting, "Keep low! Use the spray as

U. S. Coast Guard, Official

U. S. Troops Go over the Side into Assault Boats for the Bougainville Landing

Manned by a Coast Guard crew and filled with battle-equipped Marines, one LCVP (Landing Craft, Vehicle and Personnel) has just got under way, headed for the rendezvous circle. Following a schedule like a railroad timetable, this boat and others will charge the beach in waves (page 8). The 36-foot craft, designed by Andrew J. Higgins and made of wood, is armored on the sides and has a steel ramp. In the background two larger LCMs (Landing Craft, Mechanized) with grill ramps, stand by for tanks or vehicles.

a shield from the flames. Move in slowly, heads down."

Gradually the white fog smothered the fire as easily as snuffing a candle.

Walking past the docks, we saw lines of green- and gray-clad landing craft, each kind with different lettering.

"Won't you explain the alphabet names for landing craft?"

Alphabet Names Tell Landing Craft Uses

"That's simple," he said. "The letters describe what the vessels are designed to do. For instance, LST stands for Landing Ship, Tank. An LST is a large ocean-going ship which carries tanks and vehicles across the seas and lands them ready for action" (p. 2).

Veterans have many pet names for LSTs, depending upon the frame of mind. On the way over, Large Slow Target and Long Slow Trip are popular, but after "dishing it out" proud crewmen call them Last Stop Tokyo.

"There is also the new LSD, a Landing Ship, Dock, which can transport and repair landing craft in its 'stomach'," my guide continued. "It is a big ship, 457 feet long (p. 17).

"Still in the hush-hush stage is the new LSM (Landing Ship, Medium) combining features of the LST, LCI(L), and LCT(6). It's much faster than the older designs and will carry tanks and vehicles."

"But what about the LCs? Most landing craft names begin with those letters," I asked.

"That's easy! 'L' of course stands for Landing and 'C' for Craft. When we speak of a craft or boat in the Navy, we refer to a vessel small enough to be carried by a ship.

" 'I' stands for Infantry and '(L)' for Large. LCI(L)s are built as troop carriers, but in recent landings some have served as gunboats, clearing beaches for the infantry. They can ferry 200 foot soldiers long distances, feed them, and put them ashore (page 7).

" 'T' refers to tanks. So LCTs are motorized barges capable of landing a number of tanks and several small vehicles. We have two LCT types, Mark V (page 30), and Mark VI (page 29).

"LCMs are small landing craft for ferrying mechanized equipment. They can carry one large tank and are fast. Big troop transports use them to ferry troops and cargo ashore (opposite).

"Those small boats over there with the ramps—the LCVPs and LCP(R)s—are vehicle and personnel carriers. They are used as ships' boats on LSTs and for landing troops too (opposite and page 8).

"There are several other small craft. LCRs are rubber landing rafts (page 9). LCCs, or control craft, guide assault boats to the desired beaches. LCS(S)s are small support boats firing rockets and machine guns (page 6). The Amphibious Force also has several seagoing vehicles. Among them are the LVT, Landing Vehicle, Tracked, developed by the Marines (page 11), and the 'Duck,' a big truck of the Army's which navigates on land or water (page 26).

"After all, the best way to learn the uses of these vessels is to cruise on them. Report aboard LCT 509 at 7 a.m. tomorrow."

Sitting next to me that night in the officers' mess was a young LCT group commander who had three Bronze Stars on his African theater ribbon. Lt. (j. g.) Hugh D. Allen was a veteran of the Tunisia, Sicily, and Salerno campaigns. He was one of the first to take an LCT(5) to the Mediterranean region. Now he is back at Solomons, teaching new officers how to handle LCTs.

"How did you get your craft overseas?" I asked.

"After my training at Solomons in the fall of 1942, I reported aboard a Liberty ship with my crew in New York," he said. "We found our brand-new LCT broken up into three sections and lashed down on deck.

"When we got to Casablanca, these chunks were lowered over the side and my crew and I bolted them together in 24 hours. Mind you, we had never tackled such a job except in textbooks, but we managed to get the 960 bolts in their proper places and nuts turned down snugly. To our surprise our little craft chugged off as nicely as you please and held together perfectly."

Turning to another lieutenant, Allen said, "Coen, tell us about how you stocked your LCT at Casablanca."

"Sure," Lt. (j. g.) R. P. Coen replied. "After we had put our boat together, we fueled and then went out to a wrecked ship at the harbor entrance. As we came alongside, big swells bobbed us up and down and forward and back. We were scared, for we had made only three practice landings at Solomons.

"While salvage men dumped jeeps, guns, trucks, and everything else on our deck, a couple of our men went aboard to pick up anything useful. We completely stocked our craft with silverware, crockery, and fancy rations from this sunken transport. LCTs were not as fully equipped then as they are now, and this salvaged food came in handy."

LCTs Won Spurs in North Africa

"For an ensign, duty as an LCT skipper is the best in the Navy," Lieutenant Allen interjected. "He has all the responsibilities and

U. S. Coast Guard, Official

This Is What the Enemy Sees When the First Wave Hits the Beach

From the bow of an LCS(S) (Landing Craft, Support, Small), the combat photographer looks back at assault boats, or LCVPs, speeding shoreward, loaded with troops. Accompanied by shelling, strafing, and bombing with live ammunition, these maneuvers on the eastern United States coast simulate invasion. In battle, the men crouch down behind the armored visor and fire rockets from the covered projector at right. Cruisers in the distance cover the landing with shellfire.

privileges of a commanding officer. His only trouble is in obtaining extras for his crew. An ensign hasn't enough gold braid!

"After a few days Coen and I headed north for Gibraltar and then, bucking terrific head seas, we steamed down the Mediterranean to Oran," Allen continued. "I shall never forget how my LCT acted in those big seas. Her bow would rise on a wave and then slam down with a mighty wham on the next one. From the bridge I could see the deck undulate like a caterpillar. Our crew had never been to sea before, yet they handled the ship like old salts.

"About this time Ensign Jesse Anderson, an LCT friend, drew the first enemy blood for our craft and won our first Silver Star. While coasting along North Africa, a big German JU 88 swooped over and dropped a bomb while the crew was at breakfast. Fortunately it missed by 200 feet.

"By the time the plane had come around for a second run, the cook and a gunner had manned the 20 mms. and opened fire. At first the bullets went wide, but then they got on and plastered the plane. It caught fire and crashed in the mountains. Later the Army brought down a section for the LCT boys.

"During the Tunisian campaign our LCTs ferried tanks and supplies along the African coast for the Army, and so we played a part in the final victory at Cape Bon.

"My LCT landed at Licata, Sicily, early in the morning of July 10. Our job was to ferry tanks, troops, and supplies ashore from big transports. On the trips back we carried Italian and German prisoners. Once we had 225 of them on deck. They were docile and glad to be out of the fight.

"For a few cigarettes they would hand over their helmets, rifles, and other trinkets to our men. The civilian crewmen of some of the big ships, wanting trophies to take home, would buy them at fabulous prices. Many sailors made handsome profits in this quick turnover of enemy souvenirs.

"After a day or so we ran short of supplies, but we soon fixed that! Transports were anxious to unload and head for home. We soon got on to this and worked it to our benefit. Coming out from shore, I would sidle up to a fat transport and wait for a hail.

"'LCT No. 15, can you unload us?'

"'What have you got to eat?' I would yell back.

U. S. Navy, Official

LCI(L) 335 Passes the Ammunition by Bucket Brigade at Rendova

This doughty little craft, commanded by Lt. John R. Powers, ran "The Slot" more than 20 times, carrying troops and Seabees in the New Georgia and Bougainville drives (page 22). Clearly shown are the two ramps and the hornlike catheads which hoist the gangways in and out. Unloaded, the LCI(L)s (Landing Craft, Infantry, Large) wind in their stern anchors and back out, like the one in right background. Capture of Rendova played a big part in the taking of the air strip on Munda Point, close by.

Beneath Bagana Volcano Assault Boats Circle in Empress Augusta Bay Awaiting Their Turn to Storm the Beaches

During the charge, helmeted Marines in green- and brown-splotched suits crouched down behind the armored sides of the LCVPs. As the boats landed, ramps dropped and Marines poured out, quickly getting under cover. Then they "snake-bellied," or crawled on hands and knees, through the jungle to capture the Bougainville air strip. Jap snipers were hiding in the trees and strafing planes tried to break through our air cover (page 24).

Salvage Crews Come to the Rescue of an LCVP Broached on the Wave-lashed, Black-sand Beach of Bougainville

Broaching, or swinging broadside to the breakers, is the terror of all Amphibious men. Washed up farther and farther by the waves, stranded craft are "duck soup" for the enemy. Besides, the beach is blocked and time schedules are disrupted (page 20).

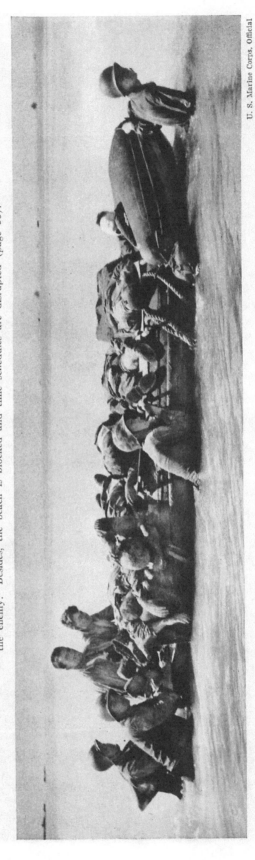

Across Tarawa's Treacherous Shelf, Tired Marines Tow Wounded Heroes on an LCR (Rubber Landing Craft)

9

A Ship-to-shore Operation Is Clearly Shown in This Dramatic Air View of the Invasion of Eniwetok

First, the battleships at top shelled and planes from carriers bombed and strafed the atoll. Then LCSs charged in, blasting the beaches with rockets. Behind them came the first waves of LVTs (Landing Vehicles, Tracked), which crawled up the beaches carrying Marines and infantry (right center). Next, successive waves of assault craft poured in. When the beachhead was secure, fat LSTs waddled in, landing tanks and cargo. Boats in center have started back to the transports for another load.

10

In This Perfectly Executed Amphibious Operation, Marines Captured Emirau in Less Than Four Hours on March 19, 1944

LSTs at sea spawned these "Alligators" (LVT1, left) and "Water Buffaloes" (LVT2, center), like guppies giving birth to young. After they had swum ashore and delivered their cargo, the amphibious tractors, or "Amtracs," returned and crawled up the tonguelike ramps into their mother ships' "stomachs." In the distance, a shore party bucket brigade passes boxes from stranded craft. At left a truck and trailer roll ashore from the bow ramp of an LCT. Emirau, a nine-mile-long arrowhead island in the Saint Matthias Group, provides the Allies with a valuable air and sea base less than 700 miles south of Truk.

11

154

It's Written on Their Faces! They Took Eniwetok in Six Hours

Tired and grimy, Coast Guard men and Marines come back to their transport in an LCVP after wiping out the Jap defenders of Engebi Island. Here they show off their Jap flag and shout, "The Rising Sun has set on Eniwetok!" When the sea is rough men must be nimble in climbing out of bobbing boats.

" 'We could spare a couple sacks of potatoes,' he'd reply. Of course, I'd cuss under my breath and move on to the next ship. Her captain would tempt us with some frozen beef or new phonograph records, and then we would go right alongside and begin loading. Sometimes the skipper would invite me aboard for a shower and a good feed. Our crews were well taken care of, too.

"Approaching Salerno, we passed in the distance the Isle of Capri. We didn't realize that big German Tiger tanks were lined up on a camouflaged road, waiting for us to get in close. All hell broke loose when they opened fire. An 88-mm. shell struck the turret of a Sherman tank on the deck right below me and blew it to pieces.

"Our flag was split by shrapnel. The quartermaster replaced it with an old one and then sat down and calmly sewed it up.

"I certainly was proud of my men during those hectic eight days when our LCT was bombed, strafed, and shelled daily. Shuttling between transport and beach, we often spotted a familiar LCT number and gave our friends a passing hail. Surprising how few casualties our landing craft had.

"After our troops had enlarged their foothold at Agropoli, south of Salerno, we went visiting ashore, while the Army unloaded our LCT. One Italian farm family I remember was particularly hospitable. They fed us a wonderful chicken dinner and served local wine. They assured us that they did not make the wine by trampling the grapes with their feet! We ate so much we got dopey. The old man and woman made us take a nap on the family's big bed."

A Day with the LCTs and Rocket Boats

Next morning I was at the dock early. Dozens of LCTs were bustling with life. Engines were coughing. Gray smoke hovered over the tightly packed craft.

I felt a deeper respect for these homely craft after the tales I'd heard the night before of their prowess in battle. To think that in a few weeks these same crews would be steering their own LCTs onto enemy beaches through bomb and shell.

The latest LCT is a rectangular, flat-bottomed barge, 105 feet long and 32-foot beam. It has "tunnels" for three propellers in the stern and deckhouses for the crew, one on each side (page 29). Forward a big ramp, upended, serves as a blunt bow. Lowered, it becomes a loading platform for vehicles and cargo.

The natural way to board an LCT, of course, is by the ramp, but when she is tied up at a dock one must climb awkwardly over the side. She boasts no fancy gangways or ladders; she is purely a utility craft.

"Welcome aboard," the skipper greeted as I jumped down to the tank deck. "I am glad you picked today. The rockettes are going to perform."

"Rockettes? What are they? LCT mascots?"

"Lord, no! They are the men who man the rocket, or support, boats. These Buck Rogerses in Navy uniforms prefer to be called rocketeers."

The skipper backed our LCT out and headed down the congested channel. Other LCTs and LCIs were getting under way too, but our captain skillfully threaded his way through the congestion.

"You handle your LCT like an expert. How long have you had command?" I asked.

"Just one week today, sir. I graduated from Midshipmen's School at Northwestern U. last month."

"But you must have had small-boat experience in civilian life?"

"No, sir. Before the war I taught high school in Missouri. I had never seen a boat before I joined the Navy. In two weeks I proceed to New Orleans with this crew to pick up a new LCT and then go overseas."

It was unbelievable, but typical of every other Amphibious craft I rode. Skippering these boats seems no more difficult to an alert American youngster than driving a car back home or riding a motorcycle.

Forming column on other LCTs, we snaked down the tricky channel to the Chesapeake, passing Solomons. In peacetime this village is famous as a fishing town and yachtsman's rendezvous. Now the liberty invasions of hundreds of blue-clad men from the Amphibious Training Base and their families all but swallow the little town.

It was a cold, snappy day and our rocketeers roughhoused to keep warm. They were a jolly, tough bunch. Among them were a few veterans of Sicily and Italy. Knots of youngsters surrounded these men, listening to yarns about rocket boats in action.

As we neared the target beach, 12 small LCS(S)s passed us. They looked like ordinary gray speedboats with armored wheelhouses and steel windshields (page 6). Each had a projector, or framework, on either side for nesting rockets.

The leader came alongside and Lt. Homer Tolivaisa, the rocket instructor, shouted, "Jump in but watch the ice on deck. The spray is freezing." Wearing life jackets, we clambered aboard the slippery, bobbing craft.

As we chugged off, the loaders carefully lifted bomblike rockets over the armored shields at the sides and placed them in the racks. They seemed as pleased as if they were setting up skyrockets for the Fourth of July. Only these rockets carried lethal fragmentation shells instead of American flags or toy paratroopers.

Playing "follow-the-leader," three LCS(S)s sped along behind us. On signal, we wheeled together and headed for the target. The lieutenant cautioned everyone to crouch down beneath the wheelhouse.

"Fire One!" he called. Instantly the rocketeer closed the switch and the rocket went off with a loud "whoosh!" There was no other noise, but a cloud of acrid smoke engulfed the boat.

Looking up, we could see the rocket wobbling and hurtling to the beach.

"Floats with the greatest of ease!" a loader commented. It struck with a dull "crump" about 100 yards short of the beach.

"That was a ranging shot," the lieutenant explained. A few seconds later he gave the order, "Fire Two—Fire Three!" Again our rockets went off with a whoosh. Sister craft fired at the same time and the shells smothered the beach around the target.

Rockets Used at Fort McHenry in 1814

"Are these the rocket boats we read about in the news from Europe and the Pacific?" I asked.

"Yes, these same boats helped clear the way for our troops at Sicily. They went in with the first waves of landing craft and cleared the beaches of machine-gun nests and strong points. It is a cheap and easy method of getting concentrated fire power. Each boat can fire in a few seconds a salvo of 24 rockets. Newer and larger support boats fire many more. Probably these men will spearhead the big invasions of Europe or the Pacific."

Rockets are nothing new. Remember the

From Wide-swung Jaws of an LST Pour German Prisoners from Italy

LSTs carry many strange cargoes. On the trip to the battle front they transport everything from donkeys and tanks to artillery, soldiers, and supplies. Returning, they bring out prisoners and wounded. Here a bareheaded Nazi officer leads off a group of prisoners. American soldiers with Tommy guns at the ready watch every move (page 24).

line, "And the rocket's red glare," in "The Star-Spangled Banner"? The British used Congreve war rockets in the attack on Fort McHenry in 1814. Francis Scott Key referred to their red trail when he wrote the National Anthem.

Back on the LCT the crew took me down to their messroom and plied me with coffee with plenty of milk and sugar. The tiny galley had an oil-fire range and family-type icebox. The two officers and 12-man crew ate at the single table, but at different servings. Informality suggested life on a yacht with a Navy tang.

"Cookie can't read a word," a boatswain's mate said. "He is a swell cook, but he runs to peas and tomatoes because he recognizes the pictures on the cans!"

Up from a hatch in the deck popped a grinning machinist's mate, like a jack-in-the-box. "Come down and see our glory hole," he invited.

Following him down the rathole, I found myself stooping in a low compartment not five feet high, painted snow-white. A whining, roaring Diesel hogged most of the space. Its high-pitched noise was earsplitting. I could not hear a word my gesticulating guide said as he conducted me through the nooks and crannies of the engine room and tried to tell me what the many varicolored ballast valves, pumps, and auxiliary engines were for.

Opening watertight doors, he took me through the other engine rooms, miniatures of the first. The temperature was high. Working conditions for the engineers must be trying, especially in the Tropics. Yet my machinist-mate guide said he wouldn't change places with the signalman up in the icy cold of the bridge for anything.

Climbing up the ladder from the starboard engine room, I found myself in the ship's head, or washroom. The captain and crew all use

A Flotilla of 14 Big LSTs Loads a Mechanized Division at Bizerte

Bound for Sicily, gasoline trucks, jeeps, tanks, and every conceivable weapon pour up the ramps and through the open bows of the big ships. Elevators take the lighter vehicles to the main deck. Skippers always put the Army's mobile antiaircraft topside so that the guns will give added protection. Most vehicles back on so they will run off headfirst. Least important go aboard early so they will be the last off. One skipper of the four LCT(5)s (right) has rigged an awning for shade.

this small room with its washbasins, hand-pumped toilets, shower, and laundry tub.

Going forward through a watertight door, I entered a living compartment for the crew and captain. Only a curtain separated the quarters. Double-deck bunks served for the sailors and for the captain and his executive officer. The captain's only conveniences were a table desk, a small ship's safe, and a camp-stool for a chair.

LCT Lands Army Tanks in Surf

It was bitterly cold and blowing hard the day the LCTs took me out to see beaching and landing Army tanks in the surf. Our little craft jumped around and yawed from side to side as she drove into the wind. When waves struck her blunt bow, the ramp clanked and rattled, spray flew, and she shimmied from bow to stern.

We paralleled the beach in single file. On signal from the flagship, we turned and headed for the big rollers crashing on the sands.

About 100 yards off, the skipper ordered the stern anchor let go, and the cable whined as it ran out behind us. Just before we hit, he stopped the engines and the ship coasted in, ramming the beach with a jar which nearly threw me off the bridge. A following sea smacked our flat stern and spouted green water and foam over the bridge, wetting us thoroughly.

Instantly the skipper sang into the voice tube, "All engines ahead two-thirds, rudders amidship. Keep a strain on the stern anchor."

Above the roar, he shouted to me, "Engines hold her against the beach, anchor keeps her stern to the seas.

"Lower the ramp," the skipper called next, and our bow dropped to the beach. Quick

In the Hot Midday Sun of Cape Sudest, New Guinea, Marines Swarm Aboard LSTs for the Invasion of New Britain

Two days later these same men in jungle "zoot suits" landed through the surf of Cape Gloucester (page 23). It took only 40 minutes for 800 men to pile up the ramp of each fully loaded LST. Antiaircraft gunners, standing by now, will soon be shooting down Jap bombers. Men sit on a broken-down Duck in center.

16

Though LCI(L)s May Roll and Pitch in Atlantic Swells, They Are Excellent Sea Boats

The sea is moderate here, yet they kick up a fuss as they plow through the water and smack their flat bottoms on the waves. From a distance the LCI(L) looks like a surfaced submarine (page 21). At night, the brilliant phosphorescent glow of spray and wakes clearly outlined the craft.

Newest Addition to the Amphibious Fleet, LSD (Landing Ship, Dock) Hides Many Surprises for Our Enemies Across the Seas

17

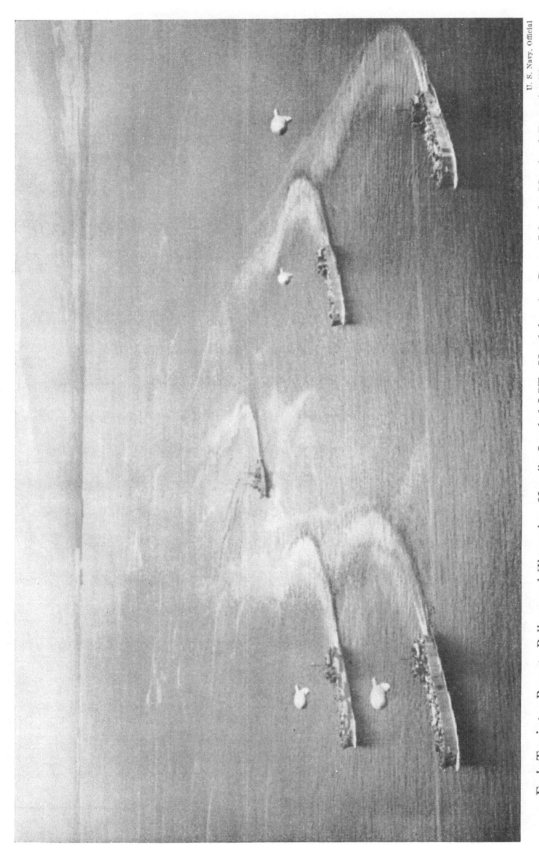

Each Towing a Barrage Balloon and *Zigzagging*, Heavily Loaded LSTs Head for the Green Islands, North of Bougainville

In this landing on February 15, 1944, American and New Zealand forces drew tighter the steel noose which is choking off thousands of Japanese marooned on Bougainville, Buka, and other islands to the south. General Douglas MacArthur said occupation of the Green Islands "completes the campaign for the Solomon Islands." Skippers claim balloons are a wonderful help to LSTs, because Jap planes cannot fly low over the convoy but must nibble at the flanks where AA guns can pick them off.

18

On This LST's Return from a Landing, Its Empty Tank Deck Became a Hospital for Wounded Marines

Big ventilators make the cargo space cool and airy. A "Green Dragon" has a sick bay in the far recesses of the tank deck; her officers' wardroom serves as operating room. Here, normally, the crew play games and dry clothes (page 24). Chains along the sides lash tanks securely to lugs in the deck.

19

Bow Pressed Against Black Sands, an LST Disgorges Men, Tanks, Trucks, into the Jungle

At dawn December 26, 1943, naval and airplane bombardment cleared the Cape Gloucester beachhead, knocking down trees and smashing pillboxes. Support boats (LCSs) firing rockets blasted remaining strong points and led the assault craft carrying Marines. Successive waves of LCI(L)s and LSTs brought in more "leathernecks," infantry, and heavy equipment. Elevator in center, fully loaded, is about to descend. Overhead, American fighters brought down Jap bombers, which fell around the beached ships.

as a flash the big Sherman tanks on the deck below came to life and chugged off, dipping and clattering down the ramp. Up the beach they tore, plowing furrows in the sand.

Suddenly the skipper pointed to the LCT next to us. A big wave had caught her and spun her around broadside to the waves. "She is broached. Now we are in for trouble," he said. "Her stern anchor failed to hold when she tried to pull off. She is helpless and we'll have to tow her off" (page 9).

Quickly our captain backed his ship out, the anchor winch winding in furiously. Big seas splashed over the stern.

We moved over directly behind the broached LCT, dropped our anchor again, and drifted slowly in. With much difficulty a hawser

was passed from our craft and secured. Then, our engines at full astern, we gradually pulled the stranded craft off.

Broaching is one of the nightmares of all landing craft, large and small. Big waves hit them broadside, washing them higher and higher up the beach. Stranding on enemy beaches throws a monkey wrench into landing operations. Successive waves of assault boats are slowed and time schedules upset.

LCI(L) Resembles Surfaced Submarine

For a week I cruised with the LCI(L)s, those doughty little craft that land our infantry on enemy beaches. We shoved off from Solomons at dawn, our seven LCIs (short for LCI(L)s) steaming in column. Quickly each picked up a creamy bow wave as she plowed coffee-colored Chesapeake Bay.

"Whenever you see a little ship with a big bow wave and white wake streaming astern, you know it's an LCI," Lt. Comdr. Archibald M. Holmes, USNR, our group commander, said. "From a distance she may look like a submarine with conning tower amidships, high forecastle, and cutaway stern (page 17). On dark nights we must be snappy with our recognition signals. Convoy escorts might mistake us for a U-boat."

Close inspection, however, quickly dispels the sub illusion. In niches on either side of the bow the LCI carries a long flat ramp, or gangway, which can be shoved out forward and dropped when beaching.

Standing down the Bay, our task unit maneuvered like big battleships in formation. The commander would send snapping flags to the yardarm and our LCIs would turn ships right, form fancy echelons, or reverse course.

Sometimes they practiced picking up mail or transferring men. One LCI ran alongside another. As the two vessels kissed, a sack of mail was passed or a sailor stepped over the side.

"How do you like the way our captains and crews handle the LCIs?" the commander asked. "Each is manned by two training crews, regular complements standing by as instructors. Not a trainee, except officers, has been here longer than six weeks. When the cruise is over, they pick up LCIs of their own at the shipyards."

As a matter of fact, not a man on the flagship, including the group commander, was in the Navy two years ago. Most of them had been in less than four months.

The new officers took frequent bearings on lighthouses and buoys, tracking our course. Sometimes their "fixes" would put us on Maryland's Eastern Shore! But they would try again and soon have us on our course.

"Where are the sailors on that LCI?" I inquired as a jungle-green LCI passed us on a turn. "I see only officers on deck."

"She is manned by officers. There are no enlisted men on board except the ship's regular crew. You see that officer on the bow, cold spray flying over him? He's the lookout. Others are at the wheel and signal hoists. After this cruise, they will be assigned new crews and then train with their men as units."

"Sound 'general quarters,'" our training captain called as the signal flags came down on the run. Instantly sailors dashed forward and aft to man the guns. "Surface target practice with the 20-mms.," he explained.

Filing past a floating target, each ship in turn opened fire. Tracers from our midship gun plastered the target in short, quick bursts. Our trainee captain, excited as a kid, shouted, "That's my squirrel shooter from Georgia. Boy, can he shoot!"

"He's a sharpshooter," replied the commander, "but what about number 5? He hasn't hit the target yet. His tracers are all over the place."

"That's my cook. He can't shoot, but he certainly can make mince pie, and that's *his* job."

With the commander as my guide, I wandered all through our little troopship. It's remarkable how much living space has been squeezed into that 157-foot, flat-bottomed hull. She has a deckhouse amidships, with a big recreation room for the crew. Here the men eat, play games, and write letters. Life jackets, helmets, and gas masks line the walls and are stuffed between the overhead beams. On one side are three small cabins for the ship's officers and the Army officers when they are aboard. The tiny wardroom, model galley, and washrooms complete the deckhouse.

Down below, an LCI(L) is divided into four big troop spaces, jammed with triple-deck bunks for 200 soldiers. On this cruise trainees occupied these quarters, officers and men sleeping side by side.

Eight six-cylinder Diesels, arranged in banks of quads, drive her two propellers.

"Our engines pull like teams of four horses," the engineer said. "If one breaks down, we can cut it out and run the others faster. Even one engine will drive the ship. While they whine in a high-pitched scream down here, you can't hear an LCI when she moves slowly.

"Many an LCI has sneaked in to a hostile beach in the darkness, unseen and unheard, until her troops jumped the enemy on shore. LCIs are ideal for leapfrogging up coasts and atoll jumping. They should be called 'ghost ships.'"

On her stern, low to the water, a big barrel-like smoke generator belches white clouds when a screen is needed. Here, too, is the powerful anchor winch, which pulls the craft off the beach in retracting.

The Charge of the LCIs

Next morning I stood high in the conning tower to watch surf beaching. Our LCI rolled and yawed in the Atlantic swells. Dead ahead huge white breakers roared up Virginia Beach. To the right and left other LCIs were charging headlong for the shore.

Are the captains mad, I thought to myself. Don't they realize that this beach is a graveyard of the Atlantic? Countless ships have been wrecked here, caught helpless on just such a lee shore. Those waves piling up on the yellow sands have rolled unmolested 3,400 miles from Spain.

Yet relentlessly on and on they rushed, bound for that maelstrom of foam.

One hundred yards out the captain let go the stern anchor and our cable snaked out astern. With a sudden shock our craft struck the beach, her bow lifting and riding up on the sand. Surf piled up under her stern and roared past her sides. Out rattled the ramps, and a sailor or two ran down to the beach and back.

"I have beached some 200 times, but I still wince every time I land in surf," the captain commented. "All my instincts tell me to turn around. Yet I must keep on, as there is no changing my mind once I start in. It's vital, too, to get that anchor out at the right instant. If I let go too soon, I run out of cable and hang from the anchor in the breakers. With too little scope, I can't use the hook to pull off when retracting."

I glanced at the other beaching LCIs. Sailors were grabbing life lines and waving their white hats at the girls on the beach. Women and children scurried out of the way as the gray steeds came galloping in.

Surprisingly, our vessel rested quietly, her stern pointing out to sea. Big waves lifted her up and down in a rocking, hobbyhorse motion.

"When the Army is with us, here's where they go ashore," the group commander said. "Carrying all their gear—helmets, rifles, packs, and gas masks—they pile from the troop spaces and run down the ramps and up the beach.

"Oftentimes we can't get in all the way. Then the soldiers must jump off the ramps in water up to their hips. If they fall, they jump up quickly and keep going, soaked from head to foot. All ashore, we retract and go back for another load."

Sailors in the bows hauled in the two ramps. The anchor engine on our fantail whined. Gradually we pulled off the beach. Well clear, our propellers took hold and we headed out, the waves rolling us down as we made the turn.

Off to Sea in a Little LCI

Again and again the ships beached, giving our two training crews thorough practice. Chief fault was a tendency to approach slowly and cautiously. Then the captain would shout, "Give her full ahead, man! Keep her moving. If you don't, the waves will take charge and you'll broach."

Beaching finished, our LCIs headed out to sea in column behind the flagship. Plowing along, the blunt bows seemed to push the whole blue ocean before them, kicking up the usual foam.

Everywhere we looked we could spot tiny Coast Guard patrol craft poking around looking for U-boats. Now and then a big silvery blimp would glide down and look us over.

Well out to sea, a Navy torpedoplane flew over, towing a big red sleeve. Our guns spit tracers and bullets into the blue sky. Most of our shots were below and behind, a common fault of beginners firing at airplane targets.

Around the table after supper in the cozy wardroom the officer instructors spun yarns about their experiences with LCIs overseas.

Lt. John R. Powers, USNR, formerly a social worker in Cincinnati, told of the adventures of LCI(L) 335, typical of all such craft in the South Pacific.

After training at Solomons, Maryland, he commissioned his craft in November, 1942, and set sail for the Pacific, one of the first LCIs to go out. After traversing the Panama Canal, he steamed in convoy nonstop across to the Society Islands, thence by way of several South Pacific bases to New Caledonia.

335's first brush with the Japanese was in the New Georgia push. At dawn she steamed into a small cove on Vangunu Island to land jungle fighters through terrific surf. Her bow stuck into the green forest. Big rollers lifted the ramps and made it difficult for the soldiers hurrying ashore. Backing out, the skipper could hear the infantry shooting in the woods.

"Did you draw any fire from the shore?" I asked him.

"No. But the surf was so vicious—10-foot waves—that I would hardly have noticed it, anyway.

"We went back to our base in the Russells, loaded again, and on the Fourth of July landed infantry and Seabees at Rendova," he continued (page 7).

"I shall never forget the fireworks that day. Sixteen Mitsubishi bombers came over and dropped their bombs just after we had retracted. In fact, the bomb pattern fell on the exact spot where we had been beached a few moments before. It was a good old Fourth-of-July celebration. Planes fell all around us. Our fighters got most of them.

"We played around close to shore, keeping as inconspicuous as possible until the sky cleared. LCIs are so small and inoffensive-looking that the enemy rarely bothers them. All the time I was more worried about the reefs than the falling bombs and AA fragments.

U. S. Marine Corps, Official

Holding Their Guns High, Marines Dash Ashore through the New Britain Surf

Breakers rolled right over the green-clad veterans of Guadalcanal as they jumped off the ramps of the LSTs. At times only their guns and hands could be seen above the surface. Yet onward they charged into the jungle to take the Japanese by surprise and capture an important air strip on Cape Gloucester. American losses were light. This landing helped seal Dampier Strait between New Britain and New Guinea. Such sandy beaches are ideal for landing vessels. But rocks, coral heads, and artificial hazards are dangerous, rip out bottoms.

"LCI 335 served as a ferry for troops and Seabees to Munda and took New Zealanders to the Treasury Islands. Altogether, she ran 'The Slot' through the length of the Solomons some 20 times, carrying thousands of troops (page 3). She took reinforcements to Empress Augusta Bay, Bougainville. There we fought the surf again. Hanging around offshore, we watched the battle and Bagana Volcano belching smoke and cinders—Nature's accompaniment to the drama going on in the jungle below (page 8).

"Standing up The Slot in November, we passed two little 'yippy' boats chugging along, loaded with Thanksgiving turkeys for our forces at Bougainville. The little YPs (converted yachts) were all alone, so they joined our convoy."

"Did many of your crew get malaria?" I asked Lieutenant Powers.

"We were exceedingly lucky; only three came down with it in our LCI flotilla," he replied. "Mosquitoes were well controlled at our base on Florida Island. Besides, LCIs usually anchor several hundred yards offshore, and malarial mosquitoes don't fly far. We sprayed our ship regularly. The only time we were really bothered by mosquitoes was when we landed soldiers at dusk or dawn." *

"What sort of food did you have?"

"We ran out of fresh supplies during the month we were at Rendova. We got along on the ship's dry stores, mostly luncheon meat. Once we went ashore and shot two wild bulls. The meat was fresh but very tough."

"Did you carry many wounded?"

"No, LCIs are not equipped for carrying stretcher cases. But we did bring out many walking wounded and fatigue cases."

Next morning when I hit the deck the ship was rolling and tossing like mad. Snug in my bunk, I had felt no motion. After breakfast I reeled down the corridor and climbed the ladders to the conning tower. The wind was not blowing too hard nor were the seas excessive, yet our LCI bounced around like a Toonerville trolley. Her bow would run up on a wave and come down with a smack on the next one. She shook like a dog (page 17).

LST—a Floating Tunnel

Back at our anchorage, the commander signaled an order to "nest up." We dropped our stern anchor—LCIs often moor by the stern—and the other craft ranged up alongside. A slight swell was running and the little ships rolled and bumped in comradely fashion. Officers and men were elated that training was done and soon they would be masters of their own LCIs.

Take a section of New York's Holland Tunnel. Put a bow and stern on it. Give it engines, propellers, and rudders. Add a bridge for the captain and you have an LST, or Landing Ship, Tank.

Of course you would have to add a few details such as a big ramp and bow doors which swing open like a garage, surround this floating tunnel with living compartments for the crew, and cover it like a porcupine with bristling AA guns.

But essentially that's the picture I got when I stood in the mammoth, white gleaming tank deck of an LST. Even the terrific roar and foul smell of a tunnel are there when huge ventilators suck out gases and big Sherman tanks whine and clank down the ramp (p. 19).

"Here's the natural place to begin a tour of an LST," said the Coast Guard skipper. "The tank deck is her reason for being. Around it centers the life of the ship.

"Here the men dry their laundry, play pingpong and basketball, toss baseballs, roughhouse, and do much of the ship's work," he explained. "When not carrying tanks and trucks, this vast space may be piled high with Army supplies, gas drums, telephone poles, ammunition—in fact, anything an army in the field may need. LSTs have even carried horses and mules. One skipper I know ferried a thousand Nazi prisoners across the Mediterranean" (page 14).

Scurrying up and down the tank deck, men were busily stacking and carrying boxes of dry stores, like a parade of leaf-cutter ants. As I watched, a little truck, like a cross between a jeep and an elevator, picked up a stack of canned peaches and whisked them down the deck, depositing them in front of a storeroom door.

"That's our Handy Andy," the skipper explained. "It saves many man-hours of work. All our men have to do is to stack the boxes and Handy Andy does the rest."

Every operation on an LST speeds loading and off-loading. If the enemy is bombing, strafing, and shelling the ship, she must be got off the beach in a hurry. Imagine completely unloading a big cargo ship in 45 minutes! Yet that's not unusual for an LST when she starts her tanks and trucks rolling down her ramp.

"Come forward and see the bow doors and ramp," the skipper said.

As we approached, the bow began to open like a secret door. Noiselessly, with no one

---

* See "Saboteur Mosquitoes," by Harry H. Stage, and "Life Story of the Mosquito," by Graham Fairchild, in the NATIONAL GEOGRAPHIC MAGAZINE for February, 1944.

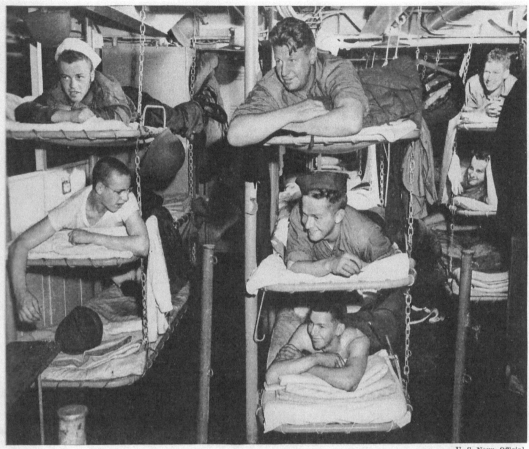

U. S. Navy, Official

A Sailor's Home Is His Bunk

On it he keeps his hammock, mattress, blankets, and many of his belongings. In addition, he has a small locker for his clothes and trinkets. While the crew space is crowded on an LST, living conditions are as good as on a big man-of-war. Triple-deck bunks fold up during daytime to make room for mess tables and recreation. Soldiers live in narrow compartments on either side of the tank deck and have their own toilets, mess tables, and bunks.

apparently operating it, the ramp swung down on its hinge until it stuck straight out in front of the ship, like a giant's mighty tongue. Flanking it, jawlike doors yawned open.

"How did you drop the ramp so magically?" I asked the skipper.

Pointing to a glass window high in a corner of the tank deck, he said, "An electrician, posted in that cubbyhole, operates the bow doors and ramp. All the machinery is inside. That's the reason you hear little noise."

From time immemorial sailors have been trying to keep the hulls of their vessels watertight. Here was a skipper deliberately opening a great hole in his ship at the touch of a button!

"How do you keep water from leaking in?" I asked.

"The bow doors only streamline the hull, giving the ship a sharp prow," he explained.

"When closed, spray splashes through the cracks of the doors, but the ship is sealed by the ramp and rubber gaskets."

We climbed ladders to the ramp-control room. "When unloading tanks we station a traffic officer here," the skipper said. "Looking through the window, he controls the tanks with signals—red, amber, green. When he receives word that the ship is firmly beached, he flashes a green light and the tanks roar off the ship, clanking as they go and splashing through the water up to the beach. If a jam occurs ashore, he flashes the amber and then the red, stopping the procession."

Traffic in this nautical garage is all one way. There is no turning around. So loading an LST is like running a motion picture backwards.

Drivers need eyes in the back of their heads, for tanks and trucks must back up the

U. S. Navy, Official

No Drill This! A Nazi Shell Just Misses Army Ducks at Anzio

Here its giant geyser plumes up between columns of amphibious trucks. One loaded with box cargo is just crawling out. Spray and fragments from the blast fly over it. Empty Duck at left is about to shed its land role and become a boat like the others heading for transports offshore. Behind the fountain an LCT off-loads from her lowered ramp. Battered by the constant German fire, work-horse LCTs have played a vital role shuttling supplies to this Italian beachhead (page 12).

ramp and into the ship's cavernous depths. Yet LSTs have been loaded with some 80 vehicles in an hour and 34 minutes. And that includes time to chain the tanks to slots in the deck.

It is ticklish business if the vehicles are bound for the upper deck. Then they must back up a second steep ramp just inside the bow. Older ships use an elevator, but this is much too slow.

Walking aft, we passed through narrow troop spaces fitted with folding pipe berths and lockers. On swinging stools sailors were eating "chow" as if at a drugstore counter. Their cafeteria-style trays were piled with bowls of vegetable soup, roast beef, mashed potatoes and gravy, creamed cauliflower, bread and big chunks of butter, and coffee.

"We can serve 300 men—sailors and soldiers—quickly and efficiently," the captain said.

Farther aft we came to a large compartment filled with triple bunks, lockers, and tables (page 25). Living quarters for the crew and troops surround the tank deck like a big horseshoe.

LST Shoots Down Six Jap Planes at Vella Lavella

The main deck was cluttered with chimney-like ventilators, cargo hatches, winches, hawsers, antiaircraft guns, tubs, and much other equipment (page 3).

An LST can put up a terrific antiaircraft screen with her many guns. Six Jap planes in one day were bagged by an LST at Vella Lavella in the Solomons last August. Not bad for a squat, sluggish ferry that many consider "easy meat" for airplanes.

Taking up much of the deck were great wooden timbers, which appeared to be a ship's launching ways.

U. S. Navy, Official

Pontoon Bridges Caught the Germans by Surprise at Licata, Sicily

As this beach slopes gradually and big landing vessels can't get in close, the Germans felt it secure and left it lightly protected. But they reckoned without the Seabees, who developed these 175-foot steel pontoons. Hung from the sides of an LST, they are dropped near the beachhead and towed alongside. When the ship hits the shoal at full speed and stops, lines are cut and the pontoons float to shore under their own momentum. Here several are connected in tandem, forming a bridge from ramp to beach.

"When we go overseas we will carry an LCT on that cradle," the captain explained. "A crane will pick up the 105-foot craft as it would a toy and gently rest it on the ways. We will secure it firmly with chains and cables and then stow other landing craft on its tank deck. First, a 50-foot LCM will go in, and inside of that a 36-foot LCVP" (page 30).

"But how do you launch that pyramid of landing craft?" I inquired.

"That's a ticklish job," he replied. "At the advanced base a crane lifts out the small boats and the chains are removed. When all is ready, we heel the big mother ship down and pull the wooden wedges. The LCT slides sideways gracefully down the ways and drops into the sea. A big fountain splashes up between the two, acting as a sort of cushion. It's really very simple, and the two vessels never scrape their sides."

"Amazing! Does the LCT have to be docked to prepare her for sea?"

"No. Her crew pile aboard, start her engines, and off she chugs. She may come around immediately to the bow of her mother ship and take on tanks and cargo from the ramp. The whole maneuver is done as smoothly as a white swan launches her little cygnets from her back."

During lunch in the wardroom several officers who had commanded LSTs in the Mediterranean swapped yarns about their ships.

For the Sicily landings, a cargo of donkeys was stabled on the main deck of an LST. Tanks and vehicles crammed her tank deck. That LST became a donkey transport and tank ship all in one!

Lt. H. R. Fleck, USNR, commanding No. 386, told how his ship happened to be the first LST to land at Salerno. "Approach-

U. S. Navy, Official

Over the Side and Down the Rope Net Climb Salerno-bound Soldiers

Three or four usually go over together, lifting left legs first, placing feet on rungs, and gripping vertical strands with their hands so the man above will not step on their fingers. They are taught to keep step so they will not bump and slow the descent. Each carries his pack jammed with rations, Garand rifle, and water canteen. Overhead flies the transport's guardian barrage balloon.

ing the beach, we struck a mine which blew out 50 feet of our bottom and part of the starboard side, including a troop space. Naturally, I thought my ship would sink and headed for the nearest beach ahead of schedule. The Navy gave me a Silver Star for that, but I was only trying to save my ship!"

"Were you under fire?" I asked.

"Yes, while we landed tanks German 88-mms. shelled us for two hours until we retracted. We steamed under our own power, with that hole in our bottom, some 950 miles to Bizerte and thence to Oran. That's an LST for you. You can't sink them!

"After the Sicily campaign, five LCTs were returning to Palermo," he continued. "Leapfrogging up the north coast, they had landed tanks at vital points behind the enemy. Now they were coming back to port battered, dirty, and tired. The flagship signaled them to pass close aboard for Admiral's inspection. The LCT boys were worried but obeyed orders. As they passed the big cruiser, the band played and all hands, including the Admiral, saluted the little LCTs."

To show how an LST gets around, I quote a letter from Lt. Charles M. Brookfield, who wrote that fascinating article for the GEOGRAPHIC about finding a 17th-century British "Fourth Rate" wrecked on a Florida reef.* Lieutenant Brookfield now commands U. S. Coast Guard LST 21, which he calls *Blackjack Maru.*

LST "Blackjack Maru" Fought in Three Theaters

"During the past six months," he wrote in February, 1944, "the ten LSTs of our group, of which *Blackjack Maru* is flagship, have cruised over 25,000 miles, operating in all three theaters of war. We have earned two Bronze Stars on our ribbons, visited eight countries, four continents, and sailed through seven different seas. That's a record for flat-bottom 'dishpans' designed primarily for ramming the beach.

"Our crew claims this ship was the first in

* See "Cannon on Florida Reefs Solve Mystery of Sunken Ship," by Charles M. Brookfield, NATIONAL GEOGRAPHIC MAGAZINE, December, 1941.

Down the Mississippi Come Six LCTs Built Far from the Sea on Rivers and Lakes

Ferry crews bring the Landing Craft, Tank downstream to New Orleans, where they are lifted aboard LSTs and sent overseas (page 30). This is the newest type, called Mark VI by the Navy. Hundreds of 327-foot LSTs, too, are built inland, many sailing 2,000 miles from Pittsburgh down the Ohio and Mississippi.

history to cross the Atlantic going sideways! LSTs have such high freeboard and shallow draft that the wind blows them off the course. Our navigator computed the leeway, as in sailing-ship days, and then plotted a 'crabbing' course.

"During the Italian invasion *Blackjack Maru* and a British LST loaded two motorized Canadian regiments for the east coast of Italy. Our ship had 71 vehicles aboard, nearly half of them General Sherman tanks—a very heavy load.

"When I showed their brigadier to a room, he brushed aside my apologies for his three roommates with the statement, 'Last night I slept on the floor!' There is always much camaraderie between the ship's crew and the Army. This is due largely to the commissary department, which serves the best possible meals to our guests. Of course there is some confusion over Navy terms, but by the end of the trip the soldiers refer to the 'deck' and 'ladder' instead of 'floor' and 'stairs.'

"Off Barletta we were ordered to Manfredonia, just captured by Commandos. For safety's sake we sneaked along close to shore,

our shallow draft making this possible. As we nosed in between the break-waters, I momentarily expected an explosion from a mine. Ships in the harbor with only masts and funnels above water were not reassuring.

"Keeping away from deeper parts of the harbor where mines might be, we let go our stern anchor, nosed up to the sea wall, and opened the bow doors. Commandos gathered around to watch the Shermans clatter down the ramp.

"The British 8th Army's drive through Italy was supported by these tanks, which took the enemy by surprise. We learned later that one of them captured a German general while he slept!

"Our 75th beaching took place in Jap-disputed territory. Our orders were to land 30-ton tanks at night on a beach too shallow for us. To overcome this difficulty, we ran up as far as possible at high water, waited for the tide to fall, off-loaded at low water so that the tanks wouldn't drown, and got out when the tide came in. If the Japs had spotted us 'monumented' on the beach, unable to move, we would have been 'duck soup.'

A 112-ton LCT Is Hoisted Aboard a Mother Ship to Ride Pickaback to Battle

It will rest safely on timber launching ways, chained securely to the deck. When the LST reaches the front she will roll herself over by ballasting and slide the smaller craft into the sea with a mighty splash (page 27). This is the Mark V-type LCT, with deckhouse across the stern.

"We claim that *Blackjack Maru* and a sister ship are the first U. S. naval vessels ever to fly the Stars and Stripes in an offensive operation in Indian waters. The scene of action is probably the most remote from our shores in this or any U. S. war."

In the afternoon our 327-foot LST plodded out for beaching. Can this 2,160-ton ship really run itself aground, I wondered. Yet, like the other landing craft, she headed straight for the beach full speed.

"If you really want to get a thrill out of beaching," the captain said, "go down and climb out on the ramp."

Down many ladders and winding passages I hurried to the tank deck. Just as I arrived, the big ramp opened, mysteriously as ever.

Dead ahead I could see the beach with the tree-clad bank beyond. Wind whistled through the opening. Gingerly I climbed out on the 23-foot ramp to its tip and looked down at the ship's bow, a bone in its teeth. The waves roared like a waterfall.

"Hang on!" an officer shouted with cupped hands. And it was lucky he did, for just then the ship hit the beach and I nearly fell off. Looking back over my shoulder, I saw the tremendous monster coming down on me, its huge mouth gaping as if to swallow me. I could see 208 feet down its gullet, the tank deck.

The ship rode up the beach for about 30 feet before stopping. Sand piled around her cutwater. A tidal wave rolled up, inundating the beach.

Retracting was much the same for the big tank ship as for smaller craft. Going astern with her engines and winching in her anchor, she gradually backed off.

Leaving the ship, Lieutenant Fleck bade me goodbye with these prophetic words: "There is not a single place on earth where we can invade enemy soil without crossing water or landing on a hostile shore. Airplanes and warships clear the way, but landing craft— *only landing craft*—take our armies to the enemy."

"Happy beachings!" I waved.

Made in United States
Troutdale, OR
09/23/2024